# COSTING NOT LESS THAN
# EVERYTHING

JOHN DALRYMPLE

# Costing Not Less Than Everything

*Notes on Holiness Today*

Dimension Books · Denville, New Jersey

Published by Dimension Books, Inc.
Denville, New Jersey 07834

First published in Great Britain in 1975 by
Darton, Longman and Todd Ltd
85 Gloucester Road, London SW7 4SU

ISBN 0 232 51320 1

A condition of complete simplicity
(Costing not less than everything)
And all shall be well and
All manner of thing shall be well
When the tongues of flame are in-folded
Into the crowned knot of fire
And the fire and the rose are one.

**(T. S. Eliot** *Little Gidding*)

Our present situation is one of transition from a
Church sustained by a homogeneously Christian society
and almost identical with it, to a Church made up of
those who have struggled against their environment in
order to reach a personally clearly and explicitly
responsible decision of faith. This will be the Church
of the future or there will be no Church at all.

**(Karl Rahner** in *The Shape of the Church to Come*)

My thanks are due to Robin Baird-Smith who encouraged me to write this book, Eileen Miller and Chris Ryan who gave me valuable criticisms, and Sister Clare of Jesus who helped with criticisms, typing and proof-reading.

# Contents

## PART 3   SPIRIT

*Part One*

# FATHER

## Chapter 1

# God Absent and Present

One of the baffling things about the life of a believer is the way in which belief in God comes and goes. As a believer I hold that God is Creator of the World and so is present in every particle of his creation. I hold this belief with my mind and am ready to point to reasons why I believe it. But it is one thing to believe in the notion of an all-pervading Presence of God in this world and quite another to have a sense of that Presence. The sense of God's presence comes and goes elusively in our lives. Sometimes it is there and sometimes it is not, even though we give intellectual credence to it all the time.

Most of us could draw up a list of experiences which have led us to believe vividly in the presence of God. Everyone would have his own personal testimony, though it is well to remember that in the last analysis these experiences are incommunicable. My own list would consist in grand experiences like the sight of the Alps one winter's morning from an aeroplane, twenty thousand feet up – silent and vast, majestically independent of man; but also in the sight of tiny delicate things like a new born baby's finger nails. Both the huge, panoramic exposure and the immensely delicate 'workmanship' of the finger nail thrill me with God's presence.

God is even more thrillingly present in human relationships, and, like most people, my list of positive experiences of God would chiefly consist in the experiences I have been given of human trust and friendship. Inevitably we take love's existence for granted, but it is, in fact, an almost miraculous experience. This ability to enter into someone else's life and become an accepted partner there, coupled with the ability to let the other person enter into our life and share our inner life with us, and, accompanying all that, the mutual sensitivity two people can have for each other so that one can be completely 'affected' by the other, though remaining distinct individuals – all this seems to be something divine, because it seems to come from a different centre from the rest of life on this planet. Love can totally transform a life from the inside while the external circumstances remain the same. There is a Presence of God in that, one which it is not difficult to recognise and adore.

And yet our sense of God's presence among men can evaporate as quickly as it came when we are confronted with all the ugly facts of life in this world, both the ugly facts we read about in the papers and see on television at one remove, and the ugly facts in our own lives. Here again every reader will have his personal list of disillusionments and despairs which have caused him to doubt if God exists: private events like the breakdown of trusted friendships, public events like the awful massacres, torture, looting, gross inhumanities which happen all around us and which are, alas, not invented but only exposed by the media. The evening news on television can be a bad period for faith and prayer. A journey through the Ballymurphy Estate in Belfast one January afternoon in 1974 vividly summed up for me this tale of misunderstanding, broken trust and failed love among men. I found fear and conflict in empty, barbed wired streets. In the

Falls Road I came across a patrol of young British soldiers. The soldiers passed a group of young 'provos' leaning against a wall. These watched the patrol go by with unconcealed dislike. Both sides looked frightened. I knew it was a long six hundred years of history which had brought these boys, who had never met, to hate and kill each other. It was not their wills, but some malignant Force from the past, which was filling the streets with hate. It was a painful effort to make the transition in my mind from what I saw to what I believed about God's presence in the world.

This chapter is not meant as a proof that God exists. It is meant to underline the fact that in terms of belief we carry round with us two sets of experiences about God which are contradictory. There are the experiences like friendships, loyalty and beauty which reassure us that God is present in his creation. But there are sharp experiences which make that belief seem a hollow joke. As we move through this world we can at times 'touch' God very nearly and all is wonder and joy. But there are the other times when we doubt if talk of such a Being has any meaning. Wonder and gratitude to God one day is followed by bewildered, agnostic despair the next.

The truth is that this world simultaneously reveals and hides God. If it only revealed God then everyone would recognise that he existed. If it only hid him, we would all be unbelievers. One side of the coin is that there are many sincere people who experience only a world which hides God. Even when they would like to, they cannot square their experience with belief in a deity. But the other side of the coin reveals an equally sincere band of men and women who believe firmly in God's abiding presence in the world and live joyfully in that presence.

12

It is a lasting consolation for them. In between these two sorts are the believers who have experienced the divine presence, but are not blessed with a continuous sense of it. Many treasure past moments in their life when they *knew* that God was there, and for the rest of the time make do with the memory of those moments bolstered with faith. They need that faith to tell them that God exists, during those bleak times when the absence of God is an all-pervading 'presence'. Creation simultaneously hides and reveals the Creator – that paradox is at the heart of belief. It makes sense of the simultaneous success and failure of world religions. Nearer home, it makes sense of the uncertain grasp we have on our own religion, now believing in 'it all' fully, now assailed by doubts which can also be total.

One way of describing this world which both manifests and hides God at the same time is to call it the sacrament of God. That is what sacraments do. They reveal but also hide. On the one hand they are signs which speak of God's active presence and so can be said to reveal him. Sacraments are veiled epiphanies, mysterious manifestations of God's presence. But, on the other hand, sacraments are not themselves God, but only signs pointing to him. Moreover they do not always point plainly – they have to be read. They have to be examined for their message and do not always yield it straight away. This is how the created world appears to believers: as a sign of God's creative activity which has to be read. If we read the sign correctly, then we recognise God's active hand in everything around us and our lives are on the way to being charged with mystical meaning. But we can easily read the world wrongly and miss the hidden presence of God. In these moods we see only the observable world and nothing else. This 'sacramentality' explains why, for some, life in this world is empty of significance, however enjoyable or active, while for others even a dull life can be full of meaning though to the outward observer it looks drab and unsuccessful. The first group have seen a world without God. The second group have 'caught' the same world revealing his presence and his challenges.

For both kinds of person, in all their experiences, God exists nevertheless. He is antecedently present and does not have to wait for man's acknowledgment. Some may believe him to be present. Some may deny it. Independent of both reactions, he is there. Holy people have the effect of being able to communicate this sense of God's real presence to other people. More than any other members of creation they reveal the hidden holiness of God to the rest of us. Their lives are shining manifestations of the Ultimate Goodness beneath all the evil in the world. When you meet them they give you hope. Saints are hope-bearing characters.

One such to me a few years after my ordination as a priest was Aggie. Aggie hid God's presence on first acquaintance because she was an old drunkard who led a disorderly life. She shared her tenement room with an unsavoury character called Paddy who was not married to her and was in and out of prison for breaches of the peace. Paddy led Aggie astray, because she only drank when he was around. She was much happier, and stopped her drinking, when he was not there. So I tried to persuade her to refuse to have Paddy back when next he 'came out'. Although she did not really like him, she rejected my suggestion. At first she would not say why, but eventually she confessed that it was because Paddy was barred from every lodging house in the city and had nowhere to go.

This was because he was an incurable bed-wetter: so Aggie gave him hospitality. Aggie took pity on him. Each time she did so, her drinking and rowdying began again. I once found Aggie with a bundle of washing, coming from the house of an old man who lived two streets away from her. She had taken pity on him, too, as his wife had died a year before and she came to see to his washing every week. Aggie was in no sense a canonisable saint, but she revealed God's warmth and kindness in her own heroic warmth and kindness. She gave me hope. The irony of it was that she thought of herself all the time as a hopeless sinner. That seems to be the way the hidden God works.

*Chapter 2*

# The Occupation of a Saint

It is easy to say that holy people are people who reveal God's holiness to the world. It is not so easy to attempt to live that holy, revealing life oneself. But all talk about holiness would be useless if we thought that it was some-thing for other people, not for ourselves. Holiness is the aim of all believers, because it is open to all believers and is, in fact, merely the state of taking our christian beliefs seriously. Baptism does not call us to a second class, run of the mill kind of christianity with an option later, should we feel like it, to turn it into the first class variety which we call holiness. Baptism calls us all to 'the occupation of a saint'. Whether grace succeeds in us or not, we have been called.

There is of course an understandable diffidence in us to claim that we are aiming at sanctity. It sounds ridicu-lously conceited. Few people feel comfortable with the idea of sanctity. The comments I got from people when I said I had been asked to write a book on holiness bore this out. They ranged from a puzzled silence to nervous laughter. Behind these reactions was a reluctance to talk about holiness, let alone make it the aim of one's life. It would indeed be conceited to aim at personal sanctity if it were our idea; but it is not. The call has come from God, not ourselves. That being so, there is, if we examine it, more pride than humility in the disclaimer that sanctity is not for us. It is the ideal given to us and made possible by grace. To refuse it is not humble, but proud.

The occupation of the saint is to disclose God's presence in this world. Disclosing God is done in many different ways. Among thinking people, for instance, it is a question of the really hard work that goes into making the truth about God, worked out in former ages and therefore in language that no longer convinces, truly convincing to people today. It is not good enough, because it is lazy and cowardly, for the christian thinker to go on repeating truths about God and the Church in the thought forms of a superseded age. There have been times when doggedly clinging to traditional expressions was the way to be faithful to God. But for christian thinkers this age of cultural change is not one of them. The highest charity to non-believers today is to attempt to put our traditional beliefs into modern language. It is also a matter of courtesy. The bleak, take it or leave it repetition of old formulas of Truth is not the occupation of a saint. New formulas have to be found for the old truths. The saintly Pope John recognised this when he opened the first session of the Vatican Council. The intellectual apostolate is for a thinking person one of the ways of being holy.

Whether we are intellectuals or not, the chief manner in which we disclose God to our contemporaries is by our lives. Our lives speak loudly, more loudly than our speech. It is all too easy to speak frequently about God but somehow not to be aware of his presence in our lives. Speaking about God like that is impersonal, dry and theoretical. But the man who is aware of God as a presence in daily living cannot be dry and theoretical about God. For him God is an active presence. Consequently the whole of his day is a partnership with the deity. There

17

is a hidden dimension, giving what amounts to infinite significance to everything he does. To meet a person like that is to sense this hidden presence and to be drawn to it. (The divine presence is simultaneously hidden and revealed in the man, who is thus mysteriously a sacrament to his contemporaries.)

We sense the hidden presence of God in people in many different ways. In Aggie I sensed it as an uncouth but mad generosity to her neighbour. Padre Pio conveyed a sense of penetrating wisdom which was not of this world. People queued for days to go to confession to him because they felt they were meeting God in him. It was Ars all over again in postwar Italy. Teresa of Avila seemed to get more human and feminine as she went on, but her contemporaries caught that sense of divine presence in her. (Even in the midst of her least defensible activities!) To give this indefinable quality in holy people the name *numinous* is to lift it too much out of everyday life. I have preferred the adjective *sacramental*, because it allows for the simultaneous hiding/revealing element in saints, which makes them terribly ordinary and terribly extraordinary human beings at one and the same time.

Although from the outside it is clear that holy people (like Padre Pio and Teresa of Avila) give a marvellous witness to God, in fact give 'a good example', from the inside this aim is probably totally absent from their minds. Their concentration is on God and other people, not on themselves. They are not concerned with 'giving witness', but with loving God and caring for the world. In Christ's day the people chiefly concerned about witness and example were the Pharisees. They performed their deeds in public for men to see. They had got caught up in themselves and could not break out of their religious

18

circle. Saints have been people who did break out of that constricting circle, because they were devoted to needs outside themselves and had no time to spare on their witness or 'image'. The paradox of sanctity is that it is attained by people who do not think about it. We are very conscious of the holiness of the saints, but they are not. They just try to find God's will, and carry it out. Their aim is not 'sanctity', but loving God and men.

One last quality that holy people have, and it stems directly from their awareness of God, is serenity. They spread peace, not tension. They are not afraid. They trust in God. Consequently they face all human situations with an ultimate calm, even when they are naturally anxious or sensitive people, and even when they are on the rampage for God as holy people sometimes are. This calm does not come from an indifference to pain, or from stupidity. It comes from the intense awareness that God is present and that, being God, He is caring for them and strengthening them in the midst of calamities and disasters. The saints' sense of God's presence gives them a deep serenity which lasts through all the 'frontier situations' of their life. They realise, with a real assent which comes from their continuous companionship with God, that God is God and eternal, while human fears are small and transitory. We may not avoid suffering and humiliations in our lives (our fears stem from trying to avoid those two usually), but with God beside us we know that all suffering and humiliation is purposed by him, and so bearable. In the end nothing matters except God's purposes, and if they include our pain from time to time, well, that is a matter for adoration and thanksgiving, not escape. In the end to adore God is what we are here for, and it is in doing that that we find peace.

In the 14th century Julian of Norwich propagated this message of selfless trust in God for her contemporaries. She drew many people to her cell with her homely serenity and wise advice. She explained 'He said not "Thou shalt not be troubled, thou shalt not be travailed, thou shalt not be distressed," but he said. "Thou shalt not be overcome".' In other words the occupation of a saint is not to makes things easier or more palatable, but to find the will of God and, whatever sufferings this may involve, do it! By this focussing of our ambitions upon the one thing necessary we are given a singleness of purpose in our life. It clears away the clutter of our multiple desires, and leaves us with a deep and lasting peace as we rest in God's will, even when that 'resting' involves much activity.

## Chapter 3

# The Divine Presence is Personal

So far I have referred to God in an impersonal way as the divine presence. It is time to give God his christian name, which is Father. This makes him personal. There is a positive challenge to the believer in that revelation. As a believer, I am asked to be aware in my daily life not just of a constant divine presence which I can refer to, but of a personal presence. This is the presence of a God who, because he is called Father, takes a personal interest in what happens to me and in what I do, and who has a positive will for me at every juncture of my life. He is not present passively, but actively. The divine presence in my life is God the Father *relating to me*.

All christians would give their assent to the proposition that God is our loving, ever-present Father. It is plainly what Jesus taught and the Church has propagated it ever since. The holy person is the one who goes further than giving it a notional assent in his mind. He actually sets out to arrange his life as if it were true. He responds to the marvel. He therefore sets up a constant conversation in his daily life between himself and his divine Father. He does not wait for special moments and special places in order to pray, but prays all the time. He 'walks with God'. In the midst of his daily occupations he talks and listens to God, because he knows that God is present. This is not as odd or as 'pious' as might be supposed.

After all, in our daily lives we carry on an interior conversation with ourselves all the time, as we observe what goes on around us and note our reactions to people and people's reactions to us. It is what is involved in having a consciousness. Constantly at the back of our minds we are talking to ourselves, reviewing our hopes and fears, making plans. Walking with God simply means that we share this consciousness with God, and so carry on our interior conversation not just with ourselves, but with the Father! This turns our inner life into prayer. There is, for instance, a noticeable difference between the thought 'I am finding this person difficult' and the quick prayer 'Lord, he's difficult. Help us two through it'. The first thought is me talking to myself; the second is me talking to God, that is, praying. Which is the truer response to life's situations? The christian believer says: the second, because God is really present to our consciousness; so to act as if he were not present is more ridiculous than to act as if he were. The person who practises the presence of God is living more really than the one who does not.

This practice of constant interior prayer does not withdraw us from secular life or turn us into dreamers. If anything, it makes us more alert, because we respond with greater alacrity to a situation in which we believe God to have a hand than to a situation where we think we are merely by ourselves. The practice of the presence of God makes us more responsible. It also follows that, when taken seriously, constant interior prayer adds a new, exciting dimension to life. It makes daily life greatly more exciting, because more personal. We are never alone, but always with the Father. We can rest in his presence even while we go about our business. Whatever the anxieties on the surface, deep down we can be utterly at peace with

God. This is the key to christian serenity.

I suppose there are as many ways of describing this interior relationship with God the Father as there are experiences of it. It depends on the person and on the culture he lives in. The trouble with many of the classic christian descriptions is that, having been written in the past, they seem to speak a different language from ours today. Consequently, instead of helping, they can hinder our chances of understanding. Some descriptions, however, speak to us across the culture gap and are useful for all time, because they are simple. De Caussade's phrase 'abandonment to divine providence' is one of those. De Caussade's teaching is that sanctity does not consist in any complicated plan or practice. It is a beautifully simple thing. It consists in discerning God's loving purpose for us every moment of the day and then abandoning ourselves to putting it into practice. Or rather, it means abandoning ourselves to *him* every moment of the day and living in that joy. Whatever the occupation of the passing moment, be it secular or sacred, be it humdrum work like ticket collecting, consciously caring work like nursing, or prayer itself, we can give ourselves to God through it and find his presence in it. All day long we can walk with God and talk to him. It is very simple. All the time he is relating to us. All we have to do is to relate back!

A difficulty for us today over the language of the mystics is the apparent passivity involved in their phrase 'abandonment'. It conjures up a picture of devout christians doing nothing when they should be doing something, sitting around cultivating their abandonment when they should be caring for others, thirsting for justice, attempting to change the world. Worse still, we begin to suspect a plot behind the stress on passivity, a plot to keep simple people docile, remembering Marx's phrase about religion being the opium of the people. But passive, docile behaviour is not what is meant by being abandoned to God's will. De Caussade himself said 'When the divine order causes us to act, holiness is in activity'. In other words we are not being called to be passive about what we do. Nor are we being invited to abandon our responsibilities. Most of the time the Father is expecting us to be doing something, and to be doing it responsibly. This is how he relates to us: by having a purpose for us to do. Whether it be bringing up a family or doing our work in society, there is no room for passivity. Christian living means we are expected to assume responsibility, not abandon it. Where, however, we are expected to be passive and docile is in the *way* we cooperate with the Father's will: not fussing or trying to alter it for our own purposes, not holding back or trying to dodge it in some way, but completely accepting it and cooperating to the full. This means cultivating a personal relationship with the Father interiorly which is one of yielding to him in all we do. In yielding to our responsibilities we find God our Father. He is behind them. Abandonment is the right word here, because it challenges us to make our relationship to God a total one, a surrender with no conditions. This approach calls for all the courage men possess and is in no way a soft or easy option for people who give in easily.

Holiness, then, means taking God the Father seriously and not escaping the reality of the situation by trying to remain neutral towards him. The divine presence in our life is not a neutral thing, but the insistent call from a personal God to discover, then do, his will. This is an inescapable challenge if we take time to think about it. The tragedy is that we do not often take God's fatherhood seriously and so do manage to escape from the challenge. Not to escape, but to face up to it means living in a starkly simple relationship of complete abandonment to God our Father. Saints are people who do just that.

Holiness, therefore, consists firstly in personally relating to the Father in the depths of one's being and only secondly in conduct, in things we do. This is an important christian truth. The Kingdom of heaven proclaimed by Christ was not primarily a programme of social and ethical thought – 'This is how you must behave'. It was primarily an acknowledgment of God as *present* and making demands upon his followers – 'God is your loving Father!' 'The Kingdom of Heaven is here!' Christianity demanded a personal response to God as Father. What was required was a conversion to God, a radical decision to belong to God and follow Jesus. John the Baptist's and Jesus' 'Repent!' was not an invitation to draw up a list of past misconduct and concentrate on future good conduct. It was deeper than that. It was a call to put faith in the leadership of Christ, a call to a personal adherence to God whose 'reign' was now beginning. Good christian conduct was also demanded, but as a fruit of the initial, 'mad' surrender, not as the act of surrender itself. There was no blueprint for action, only a call to react promptly to a Person. Working out the subsequent moral response came later but was not foreseen in any 'programme'.

Another way of putting this is to say that christian holiness is not a Moralism but a Mysticism. The right conduct is the product of the right relationship to the Father. The latter comes first and is central. Abandoning myself completely to the Father is what most matters. The pursuit of virtues and the avoidance of vices only

25

make sense as ways of being abandoned to the Father, not as ends in themselves. This is clear from the Sermon on the Mount. The sermon is full of ethical advice, but it is secondary. The central advice of the sermon is to try and please the Father 'who sees in secret'. A prompt and eager relationship to God, not a definition of conduct, is the chief issue. This christian balance between the primary mystical relationship and the resulting secondary virtuous life is evident in everything St Paul wrote, too. For him good christian living comes from having the right relationship in Christ to the Father. St Paul's writings contain many ethical prescriptions but they are to be found at the end of his epistles. They come not so much in the form of exhortation as in the form of the inevitable fruits of his readers being in Christ. Concentrate on the marvellous truth that you are interiorly united to Christ and the rest will follow, is his clear message. 'When a man is in Christ, there has been a new creation.'

What I have said above presents a challenge to us today. In this century we have experienced what amounts to an ethical explosion. After years of taking himself and society for granted, man is now intensely concerned with how he relates to himself (psychology), how society relates to itself (sociology), how society can be improved (politics). New discoveries have been made and we now know so much in those three fields that our former knowledge looks paltry. Psychology, sociology, politics make us yearn for and work for perfection in all these fields. There is an admirable moral determination in modern man, some of it christian, some of it not, but all of it very earnest for improvement.

This moral determination has spilled over into Catholicism, especially since Vatican II, which taught us to look for help from the modern sciences. The result has been a widespread ethical perfectionism in the Church. I have been on retreats with religious communities where there was an intense pre-occupation with structures and right relationships in the light of the latest updating documents. I have also attended summer schools given over to the right way of performing liturgy, praying with the Scriptures, being responsible in community, being fulfilled. At first sight, all this energy seemed to be directed into very proper channels. But on reflection I realised it stopped short of the point. The point is not really the means used to please the Father (christian behaviour) but the actual relationship of pleasing him (christian conversion). Too much concentration on seeking perfection in behaviour (whether pre-conciliar or up-to-date) leads us to a dangerous spiritual selfcentredness. We become totally absorbed in how to act, relate, discern – totally absorbed in fact, in our own poor selves. This in turn can lead to increased anxiety about how we are performing, whether we are behaving correctly, whether we have 'got it right'. Then we are tempted to discern and evaluate all over again and a sad circle of zealous anxiety has begun. Christian holiness breaks out of that circle by abandonment to the Father. All trust is placed in him and spiritual anxiety is placed firmly in the background. Christian holiness is a challenge to relate to the Father in such a way that we decrease in our consciousness while he increases. On the way to this, admittedly, a controlled amount of behaviour evaluation can be a help. But the means should never be turned into the end, and the aim of christian living is quite simply union with God, not correct behaviour.

27

In saying the above I am claiming that the relationship to the Father which Jesus propagated as the basis of the new life is not a 'mythological' part of the Gospel which we can afford to drop, since it is out of keeping with how modern man thinks. I think it is the centre truth of the Gospel. If we are tempted to admire the christian virtues (justice, honesty, love) but to discard the christian teaching on God as Father, we are being tempted to destroy the heart of the Good News. Christian holiness is the attempt to live one's life in obedience to the Father's will, understood as a personal command. The pursuit of perfection follows from that as the commanded way of obeying. It is not an end in itself. Christian holiness is relational not perfectionist.

A good way of understanding the relational element in christianity is to examine what sin is. When I commit a sin, for instance, an act of dishonesty, I can review that act in various different ways: as transgressing the christian code, as letting myself and society down by failing to live up to my standards, as acting inauthentically. The saint will admit the truth of all three descriptions, but will see what he did in a different way. For him his act of dishonesty was an offence against God, his loving Father. Everything else fades in comparison to the felt enormity of that personal offence. It is not that he has failed in his pursuit of perfection which worries him. It is that he has displeased the Father. What he now wants is forgiveness from a Person, not good resolutions or psychological readjustment.

## Chapter 4

## The Secularist Difficulty

The secularist difficulty is this. 'You should not talk about God as a person outside this world, guiding it with his will. To talk like that is to regress to a pre-scientific manner of speaking, animistic in tone. Pre-scientific man gave personalities to forces which were outside his control, and thought of those "gods" as directing life on this planet by sending natural disasters and "punishing" and "rewarding" men through the events of history. Odysseus interpreted his many adventures before he reached home in terms of being attacked by a hostile Poseidon and favoured by a friendly Pallas Athene. But it did not *really* happen like that. It was just the way men had in those days to describe natural forces which they could not understand or control. It was a way of making those forces somehow intelligible to men, the only way at that time available to tame the universe.

'The men who wrote the Bible were equally ignorant of the workings of natural phenomena and equally powerless before them, so they too described events in terms of God's favours and punishments. Jesus was a man of his own day and also spoke that language. His central insight was that the heart of the universe is benevolent, not malignant, and he chose to describe that fact in terms of a loving Father who created the world and watched over it, sending the rain upon the "just and unjust" alike and doing other personal acts through the events of nature and history. This use of personalist images like God the Father, or the angels, was pre-scientific man's way of filling the gaps in his knowledge and in his competence, both of which were extremely limited. Man, come of age, in this scientific era, no longer has to use the concept of a divine person watching over the world in order to provide intelligibility to nature. He already knows a lot about how the world works. The areas of remaining ignorance, he feels, will give way to scientific research without recourse to the interventionist God of the christians.'

This is a serious objection, one that, if true, would make nonsense of the description of the saint I gave in the last chapter – the one who whole-heartedly abandons himself to God as Father – or at least would make him out to be a backward-looking character who has not come to terms with modern knowledge, a left-over from a past age, who runs away from secular challenges.

The difficulty can only be answered by going along with scientific knowledge and by accepting, not denying, that there is a natural explanation for every phenomenon in life, and agreeing there is no need to think up an interventionist God to explain the unexplained events in life. The God christians believe in, the loving Father of the Gospels, is however, not like that. He is our loving Father but, miracles apart, he is not interventionist. He does not work in the world apart from secondary causes, but he exists behind them and is at work *all the time* through them. God heals people through doctors and nurses. He teaches us through schools and universities. If we ask him for favours we know he will answer through natural events. We are asking him to act within the laws of his creation, not outside of them. In other words, God and man, in the christian scheme of things, are not rivals, as if God has to rest while man is working, and man has to rest while God intervenes. They are not rivals, but partners, operating on different levels of action as first and secondary causes of the same events. To recognise this is to recognise the autonomy of secondary causes in their own order. God and man act all the time together, but each on a different plane. To put it another way. Man's activities in this world are the sacrament of God's activities. Although in one sense they hide God's work in the world, in another sense they reveal it. Secular activity is thus not a sign of God's absence from the world but paradoxically of his dynamic presence.

Once this is understood it becomes possible to see how holiness, which I described in the preceding chapter as relating to God seriously as a loving Father, can still be that even in our scientific age. Relating to God as my Father is what I do all the time at the deepest level when I am engaged in work. Meanwhile simultaneously at the visible level I am busy relating to the natural phenomena with all the skill at my command. The two actions are not contradictory, but complementary. The saint, then, continues to be the one who, while engaged in trying to master a situation at the human level, is also engaged in yielding to the hand of God hidden in the situation. He lives at a deeper level than the immediately visible, and at that deep level is all surrender. Dag Hammerskjöld, when Secretary General of the United Nations, worked night and day for world peace at the level of international affairs, but within himself surrendered to God, as his autobiographical notes, *Markings*, show so movingly. They are the record of a busy statesman who was interiorly a mystic.

31

There is a link-up here with what was said in Chapter 1 about creation simultaneously hiding and revealing God. In so far as the world hides God, we get on with the task of mastering it and using it to our advantage. This is the realm of natural causes. In so far as that same natural world reveals God we approach our task with reverence and respect towards the presence of the Creator hidden in the events. Holiness consists in acting with complete dedication at both levels, but especially in discerning the presence of the Father at the deeper level of Creator, and acting with approriate zeal and adoration. Treating God as a loving Father hidden in this world is not, therefore, a regression to pre-scientific animism, but a serious response to the spiritual facts about this world just as science and politics are the serious response to the visible facts of the world.

In everyday life the difficulty is chiefly one of language. We use the language of natural causes most of the time. For instance we say: the war was caused by this series of events; or, this illness is caused by a germ which I now proceed to treat medically. But about the same two situations we can use the language of God's will: it was in God's plan that the war came; I am offering up the sufferings of this illness to God who sent it to me. These two languages do not cancel each other out, but are complementary. They are both true. The 'holy' language of the First Cause bypasses but does not deny the language of the natural causes. Too often in the past we have thought that the holy 'bypass' language denied the validity of scientific language, with a consequent denigration of the importance of the scientific world. All those who use bypass language, like preachers and spiritual commentators, ought to remind themselves of the importance of the world in which God works and whose laws he respects because he made them. All those who attend to natural phenomena should pause from time to time to reflect on the loving Father who creates the universe and is hidden in its workings. The serenity of the saints comes from a constant awareness of God at the deepest level even while they are fully engaged in making plans at the surface level. The secular is a manifestation of the holy, not its cancelling out. This means that the call to sanctity is among other things a call to respect the holiness of secular things, to recognise the sacramentality of the universe. Paradoxically, the way to preserve the importance of this world is to give importance to the Father God who is separate from it (though at work within it). For the believer the reason this world matters is because God who creates it matters.

*Chapter 5*

# The Mystical Difficulty

The secularist difficulty about God comes from knowing so much about how the world works that it is difficult to see where God fits in. Another difficulty about regarding God as Father and giving him a personal role to play comes from the other, the mystical, side, from people who know God enough to know that you cannot really encompass him in human terms, like Father. The difficulty here is not in finding a place for God to fit in. On the contrary his place as Lord of creation is given in adoration. The difficulty is in the too free application to God of words and concepts which really belong only to human experience. It is the difficulty and danger of anthropomorphism in talking about God. Is it really helpful, and does it give a true picture, to talk about God as a loving Father? Does it not, in the very act of trying to enthrone him as Lord, rob him of his true nature by cutting him down to human size? *Un dieu défini est un dieu fini*, the mystics say. He is not God if we make him too humanly understandable.

The short anwer to this difficulty is that human language is the only language we can use as human beings and even the mystics who claim that we can know nothing about God have to use human words to tell us so – in fact it is a feature of mystical writers that they say a great deal about not being able to say anything about God! A shorter answer still for believers is that the Bible uses human words about God, and it is from the Bible that we know that God is Father. But it would be a mistake to dismiss this difficulty too lightly because it represents an important objection and points to a real truth, namely that at the heart of christianity is a reverent agnosticism.

Language, concepts, words are the way in which human beings attempt to control the world they live in. When I am in a mess and muddle and do not know how to handle a situation, I go to a friend and talk about it. The very act of talking about it helps me to control it. I find words to explain the muddle I am confronted with. Finding the words helps me to know what to do next. If my friend, after listening, adds a few words of his own in judgment of the situation, I am even more helped to control it. Our joint judgment has domesticated the wild forces of the mess and muddle. That is how the healing sciences work. They apply words, judgments and, eventually, a whole science to enable men to tame and domesticate the unknown and frightening illnesses we suffer from. Words like manic-depressive, schizoid, inferiority complex, can be a great help to people who are labouring to understand the mysterious forces within themselves. In the same way a mysterious pain becomes much more bearable when a doctor has given it a name like sprained ligament or appendicitis. Naming the pain gives immediate hope that the situation can be controlled just because it is here and now labelled. The comfort of science has been applied to a bewildering situation.

The science of theology operates in the same way. It is man's way of trying to comprehend the wildest and most unknowable of all the forces in the universe, the Creative Force itself. We give this Force the name 'God' and almost at once a certain domestication has taken place. This mysterious, unknowable Force has been encapsulated in an easily handled monosyllable. (Before long we are saying 'My God', 'Good God', 'Almighty God' with great glibness.) Then we build up a science of God and give him many names and attributes, and elaborate his plans and actions as revealed to us in history. Following the example of Jesus Christ we call God Father. We also elaborate the appropriate response man should make to God: conversion, adoration, contrition, intercession and so on. The result is a coherent theology and a certain expectation of how God should act and what he is like. Like all sciences, theology is a taming of the situation.

That is where the danger lies. All the other sciences proceed under the perfectly legitimate supposition that it is right for man to try and master the world he lives in. Theology's initial supposition is more ambiguous. It is certainly right for man to try to comprehend and master himself as a religious being. But to try to master God, and give him names, and predict his actions, and judge his plans, and assign him a place in the universe? That is where we are in danger of going too far, because the one Force which we cannot and should not try to encapsulate and master is the Creative Power itself. In the face of that we ought to bow and be mastered, filled with awe. Failure to do that is to miss the point catastrophically:

> 'Earth's crammed with Heaven,
> And every common bush afire with God;
> And only he who sees takes off his shoes . . .
> The rest sit round it and pluck blackberries.'
>                    (Elizabeth Barrett Browning)

Theology, then, has a double task. On the one hand to go on trying to understand more and more about mankind's religious behaviour, which means delving into christian revelation and comprehending the content of christian doctrine. On the other hand constantly to keep open the relationship with God as one which we should not try to be master of, and so avoid the irrelevance of plucking blackberries round the Burning Bush. We are to keep alive in our minds a realisation that the words we use about God are inadequate human approximations. Between the human mind and the reality of God lies a cloud of unknowing. Let us not forget that. It makes all that I have said so far about treating God as Father fit into place. God can be described as Father – yes, but prayer tells us that the Reality behind our human description is infinitely more mysterious. In prayer we discover that God is beyond human words, and that it is only approximate to speak of him so 'humanly'. That is why the heart of christianity is what I have described as a reverent agnosticism.

Nevertheless, although words about God are only our human attempts to describe the mysterious reality, they are in their limited sense true. As long as we remember that our words about God fall infinitely short of reality, and as long as we do not use theology to try to control the Divinity but only ourselves, then it is right to go on using words and thinking about God. Nothing, in fact, is more worthwhile. Speechless silence is ultimately the only adequate response to God, but it has to be silence which comes after the effort to try and understand. If we lapse into the silence too soon, it could be out of laziness or lack of interest. The valuable silence is the silence which comes because words have been tried hundreds of times and failed. The story of Thomas Aquinas at the end of his life saying that his *Summa* seemed like straw compared with the experience of God he had been given in prayer is significant because the experience came after Thomas had made his huge effort to understand. The objection, then, that we cannot use words like Father about God because they are anthropomorphic is valuable when it reminds us that the reality of God is far and away more mysterious than our human concept of fatherhood can grasp. Meanwhile, however, Jesus (who himself spent mystical nights in prayer and forty days in the desert) has used this human word to describe God. What it tells us about God is an immensely valuable approximation to the actual truth and not a mere metaphor. It is the revelation that the heart of reality is personal, benevolent and optimistic. The saints are those who plumb the depths of human misery, and yet remember that. Like Julian of Norwich, in the midst of their passion they say that 'All shall be well'. Calling God Father, then, is not a facile anthropomorphism. It is Jesus' challenging proclamation about the destiny of this world, as it were, in the teeth of evidence to the contrary. It is in fact the deepest truth we know about God and this world. It is, therefore, the foundation of holiness.

## Chapter 6

# Learning from the Difficulties

The theme of this book so far has been the call to surrender ourselves to the Father in the depths of our hearts. The language people use to talk about this varies; conversion, abandonment, surrender, commitment, adoration, obedience, interior life. . . . Each word has a nuance which expresses a certain spiritual reality. But the important thing is the reality beneath all those other realities, the reality of God the Father, present to us and making demands upon us. To recognise and respond to that is the beginning of holiness. What follows afterwards is really not our business! The direction that obedience and abandonment to God takes in our lives is God's business, and has in the past taken all sorts of different forms, like living in the desert as a hermit, caring for the poor in big cities, being Lord Chancellor of England. For each reader of this book it will take a different form, but for all it will have the same starting point: facing up to God and doing what he wants. The conviction that God is a person with a will for each of us is where we all start. We cannot dodge away from that. There is no christian holiness without it.

This is the reason for the last two 'apologetic' chapters. They would not be necessary if it were easy today to make a start from the point that God is a personal fatherly being who relates to us. Just because that statement needs explaining I have taken the secularist and mystical difficulties seriously. They have to be taken seriously and not brushed under the carpet, because they are real.

Another reason for examining these two objections is that they themselves contain important christian truths. They are genuine reactions against past errors committed by christians. The paradoxical result is that by taking these reactions against itself seriously, christianity uncovers in the arguments of its adversaries genuine christian truth and so advances in self-understanding. The secularist difficulty about regarding God as a personal being distinct from the world represents a genuine defence against the all too frequent christian mistake of underestimating the importance of this world in order to magnify God. Undiscriminated talk about God and the supernatural can lead men to bypass nature and think of God acting upon the world from the outside, with a disregard for natural forces. The 'either-or' mentality sets in and God and the world are set up in opposition to each other. Then devoted christians, thinking they have to choose between God and the world, naturally choose God and begin to denigrate nature. They neglect science, avoid beauty, flee from contact with the world – all this being done in the name of a devout following of God's will. This is clearly a negation of humanity and life in this world, so the understandable secular reaction to the stark choice offered is to prefer a world without God to God without the world. This is the situation in post-Victorian Britain. A misguidedly 'spiritual' christianity has resulted in a reaction towards atheism. Furthermore the atheistic reaction contains the genuine christian truth that this world is to be taken seriously.

This over-spiritual understanding of God's relationship to his creation has repercussions within christianity too.

There arises a demand for a secular christianity. This is fine if it means a christianity which recognises the autonomy of creation and seeks to promote the importance of this world, a christianity trying to correct Victorian denigration of the world. But it becomes less acceptable when it goes further and denies the possibility of a personal God who is our Father. I have tried to show in Chapter 4 that the true christian notion is that God is personal but not in the sense of being interventionist or 'magical'. If we understand Creator and creation with a 'both-and' mentality, we will see that they co-exist as partners and that therefore secular science in this world is perfectly compatible with sacred belief in God the Father, Creator of the world. For the purposes of this book, the important truth is that holiness which commits us to God the Father, by that same act also commits us to God's world. The Creator and his creation are not rivals, but partners. Reverence for one means reverence for the other.

The second and mystical difficulty about calling God 'Father' and 'Being' also contains a defence against error in favour of truth. This time it is the error of cutting God down to human size, domesticating him and making him too cosy. Too facile talk about God being our Father might lead us to think of him in such a way that we thought we knew everything about him and had him taped! If in the past 'saints' have tended to neglect the world and be puritanical, so they have also tended to this sort of confident certitude about God and his plans. Some have been awe-inspiringly certain that they knew what he wanted and that his will and their will coincided. This has been the tendency of religious enthusiasts in the christian past (many of them ecclesiastics) who have committed devastating acts in the name of God. Not surprisingly it too has produced a reaction against christian certitude in favour of agnosticism. But here again the reaction uncovers genuine christian truth. Agnosticism about God and his plans is, in fact, fundamental to christian doctrine. An important part of the familiarity with God promoted by Jesus is the fact that the more we enter upon knowledge of him, the more we are plunged into the cloud of unknowing about the divine nature. In fact, the edge and 'bite' of christian spirituality is the fact that we are invited to call the unknowable Force behind creation 'Father' ('Abba' means 'Dad'!) even as we take off our shoes on the holy ground. In Jesus' teaching there was never any doubt that we could never fully comprehend God. Yahweh remained Yahweh. Holiness, then is not a question of being cocksure about God or complacent. It is a deeper and deeper involvement in mystery, an adventure into agnosticism, even while it is an involvement in Creation. God is mysterious and incomprehensible in his presence in this world. The mystery of God is not a mystery outside this world but at the heart of it. The saints are the people who have delved deeply into God and have delved deeply into this world, worshipping the same mystery in both.

## Chapter 7

# Costing Not Less Than Everything

You cannot be neutral about God. Once you know that he exists and is your Creator you have to respond to him with everything you have. To admit God only into a part of your life, a 'religious' part which exists alongside many other parts but has no influence on them, is not really to admit God into your life at all. The Father that Jesus Christ revealed to us and put us in touch with enters into every part of our life (he is Creator and Lord of all) and makes total demands upon us. He is, indeed, revealed in the New Testament as most merciful and understanding (the Father of the Prodigal Son) but also as *God* – asking everything from those prepared to give him everything. He did not spare his own Son in Gethsemane or on Calvary; He supported but demanded to the end. What God asked of the saints and Jesus himself, he asks of all His followers. *We* are all called to what *they* achieved.

The first step in christian discipleship, then, is a stripping bare of those interior compromises we make which help us to answer the call more comfortably without undergoing a radical conversion. Those compromises exist. We like to 'accommodate' the christian vocation to a more comfortable worldly standard. When we do that we pad out the simple message with non-christian material; we start to live with double standards. I am not here referring to sin, which is a direct saying no to the demands of God, but to all the yes-buts we offer to the call, by which we contrive to answer and not answer at the same time.

It would take too long to enumerate all the compromises by which we lukewarm christians soften the impact of Christ's demands in our lives; and perhaps it would be futile, since each disciple of Christ has his own weak areas, private to himself, where he calls a halt to his Lord's demands. Nevertheless there is one general area which I would like to focus attention upon because of the frequency with which we say yes-but when we enter it. This is the area of social conformity.

Among mankind's frequent yes-buts is the assumption that whatever God asks of us, he will not ask us to go radically against the customs of the society we live in. We presume that social non-conformism is not part of what God is going to ask us to do. But it can be! It is not inconceivable that facing up to the Father's will in my life may mean separating myself from society. This is very difficult for most human beings because we are on the whole conformist by tradition and upbringing, especially in countries where the Church is not in conflict with the State. We prefer not to be in conflict with the State and have a partly conscious, partly unconscious, horror of 'disobedience' to secular authorities. We so readily identify secular authority with God's authority and sanctity with quiet conformism. Furthermore, since the Vatican Council, catholics have been encouraged to go along with their non-catholic contemporaries, both christian and non-christian. No longer are we allowed to be 'different' as a matter of course. The Church has removed all the awkward things like the ban on mixed marriages and meat on Fridays, so we do not stick out like sore thumbs any more. This undoubtedly sound eirenicism nevertheless breeds an increasing appetite for social conformism.

We should even be prepared in our christian discipleship to be in disagreement with the authorities in the Church if God makes that demand. Thomas More in 1535 had to dissociate himself from the entire body of bishops, except John Fisher, on his road to sanctity. In the last war the Austrian peasant, Franz Jägerstätter, felt that God did not want him to be conscripted into the German Army and that to be faithful he had to refuse to serve. This involved going against the advice of both his parish priest and his bishop – a formidable thing for a mid-European peasant to do. He did so, and was beheaded by the German authorities, in complete loneliness.

I am not here arguing that everywhere on all occasions being a follower of Christ involves social nonconformism. The Gospel is not politically naive like that. Sometimes we are led to conform, sometimes to dissociate, sometimes to rebel. There is no antecedent bias in the matter. But I am stressing this particular obstacle to holiness at some length because the language we use about total conformity to God's will could lead us to think that sanctity means conformity all round. God's will cannot be identified with any institution in this world (not even the Church authorities) and we can never be told to obey a human institution and ask no questions. We must discern whether the custom or law we are being asked to conform to is in accordance with what God wants or not. Perhaps more often than not, it is. But this must not be presumed. It has to be clearly examined first. Conformity to God the Father, yes. Comformity to society? The hard

45

thing is that the former sometimes requires us to deny the latter.

All the above is only another way of saying that God enters into the whole of our life and that there cannot be one compartment which belongs to him and other compartments which do not. The christian stockbroker cannot have a stockbroker part of himself which coexists with but is not influenced by the christian part. The two have to meet – if necessary in conflict – and the christian part has to prevail. This integration of oneself under one master, God himself, is very much the business of holiness. The same applies to the christian soldier, the christian trade unionist, the christian clergyman, and so on. It is an uncompromising business!

This is what is meant by being radical. Christianity is not radical in the external sense of always demanding revolution and the overthrow of established structures. There is just as much a conservative element in it too. But it is radical in this interior sense of a conversion to the roots of the being, allowing no part of oneself to be unaffected by the demands of God, and facing the consequences of that. Without a deep inner conversion to God there is no real christian discipleship. The initial 'repent' of Jesus Christ was a call to total conversion. It was not an invitation to jog along with the christian majority, practising one's christianity as a social conformism. The response to Christ was meant to go to the roots and affect the whole of life.

Let me here enter a warning against too much adherence to 'common sense'. Common sense is a good thing. It is the pragmatic ideal of the British. But it can also be the enemy of ideals. It is, therefore, a state of mind to be treated with initial scepticism rather than ready acceptance. The good is sometimes the enemy of the best. What we admire the saints for is their startling rejection of common sense in the interests of something higher and grander. As I write, I am thinking of Aggie's hospitality to Paddy; or Charles de Foucauld's life in the Sahara. There was a mad christianity about them, and any saint you care to think of, which inspires us beyond words just because it transcended common sense. They went beyond what sensible people in the world would expect them to do. The call to holiness comes to all of us sooner or later in this form of being asked to reject the common sense good and opt for a mad best for the sake of God. It almost inevitably means taking a risk. Charles de Foucauld said 'the absence of risk is a sure sign of mediocrity'. To go back to de Caussade, his phrase 'abandonment' ought to have nothing merely soothing about it. It sounds, and should be, a call to leap into the dark, counting no costs, undertaken not for the sake of shocking or for novelty, but simply out of the conviction that it is what God the Father wants. We are, of course, all expected to look before we leap, but no amount of looking will be a substitute for the actual leap. *That* is always a risk. The reward only comes when it has been done, when we discover that in spite of all our fears and forebodings we have ended up in God's arms.

This radical conversion which the Father asks of us is not a once for all event which then lasts for the rest of our lives. There are, for many people, special moments in their lives when they encounter God and are converted. They are precious moments, for which to thank God. But such moments do not result in our immediate shortcut conversion, however much we may feel that to be so when they happen. In this life we continue to travel, never to arrive. Kierkegaard said that no one can say he is a christian, only that he is becoming a christian. Christian holiness, then, is not achieved by one radical leap from common sense to divine folly, but by a lifetime of being faithful to such conversions. As T. S. Eliot puts it, we are given brief moments of fusion with God which transform us, but they are only moments

> '. . . and the rest
> Is prayer, observance, discipline, thought
> and action.'

Earlier in the same poem he explains that the occupation of the saint is something given and taken

> '. . . in a lifetime's death in love,
> Ardour and selflessness and self-surrender.'
>                                    (The Dry Salvages)

In those few lines the poet seems to have said everything necessary. Holiness is a lifetime's pursuit and no sudden flash in the pan. It involves a slow death to self. But it is death with a purpose – the purpose being to live again a wholly new life of ardour and love for God and man. These thoughts bring us to Jesus Christ who introduced this new life to men and showed us how to live it.

# *Part Two*

# SON

*Chapter 8*

# Jesus Christ

We call God 'Father' because Jesus Christ did so and encouraged us to do so too. We ought not approach God without referring to Jesus Christ, because it is from him that our christian practice comes of regarding the Creator of the universe as Father. To have reached Chapter Eight without concentrating on Christ in a book on christian spirituality is a bit misleading, because he is the origin of our knowledge of the Father and without him all that I have so far written would not be known. The truth is that Christ is present implicitly in every christian approach to God. Sometimes, however, it is wise to let this presence remain implicit, because Jesus did not want men to centre on himself but to centre on the Father, and to regard him as the Way, not the goal of christian devotion. It is now time to concentrate on Christ, since there can be no christian holiness otherwise.

Christian holiness means taking Jesus Christ seriously. It means taking the historical figure of Jesus of Nazareth and studying what he did and said as a standard for our own living. I wonder if we realise how difficult that is? The universal figure of Jesus has been studied and written about so often since he lived that each age has virtually succeeded in producing a new Jesus, to suit its own tastes. It is difficult now to dig below the literary crust of the generations to the real man. What are we to make of a man whom 19th century writers called 'Gentle Jesus, meek and mild' and 20th century writers portray as a revolutionary leader? The byzantine mosaics of the early centuries depict Christ as pantocrator, the Lord of Creation, who looms awesomely over the apses of the basilicas, steady, confident, summoning men to judgment. On the other hand in modern show-business presentations Jesus comes over as a bewildered man like the rest of us, full of doubts about his mission, easily hurt. Those who write about Jesus Christ tend to project upon him their own needs and desires and not be entirely objective. Nevertheless each honest presentation contains some truth. All we can do is remember that Jesus is a many-sided and not easily comprehended character. Furthermore, he belongs to the history of the human race, so an enormous amount has been written about him, much of it contradictory. If we turn to the Gospels for the original picture, we have to remember that even they belong to the literary crust, so they do not give a completely objective account of the man. All this is not to absolve us from taking the historical figure of Jesus seriously, but merely to point out the difficulties.

The 20th century European follower of Jesus Christ has to contend with further difficulties in trying to understand Jesus Christ. Between him and Jesus lie three main gaps. First there is the culture gap. Ponder for a moment who Jesus was. He was an itinerant, middle eastern, religious preacher. He was socially and culturally miles away from us. He was a country 'arab' whom we might well avoid having in our homes. (We might well avoid mixing with his mother, too.) In other words, there is a very considerable culture gap between Jesus and the readers of this book. It is not, of course, unbridgeable, but the first step in bridging it is to be aware of it. This means strenuously purging our minds of the assumptions that unconsciously make Jesus the same class and culture as ourselves. To be frank, many of us would not be comfortable having him in our families and mixing with our friends. He was a provincial man from Nazareth. His social appearance was not modern European. Gentle he may have been, but he was also an uncompromising figure in the line of the Jewish prophets. In calling ourselves 'christians' we are submitting ourselves to that sort of person as our teacher.

Besides the culture gap between us and Jesus, there is also the knowledge explosion of the modern era. Jesus lived before that, and so was ignorant of a hundred things we take for granted. The christian takes as his master a man who in 20th century terms, was ignorant, because he lived before the age of modern discoveries in all branches of learning – not just mechanical discoveries like the internal combustion engine, but discoveries in the human sciences like politics, psychology and sociology. 'Jesus lived before the days of a cash economy,' said an economist to me, as we discussed the Sermon on the Mount. Listening to the words of Jesus we thrill at the wisdom there which is valid for all time and deeper than mere knowledge, however spectacular. But for the sake of truth we ought to recognise that the master we choose to follow lived in a relatively ignorant culture by modern standards and was a man of his age. If we do not remember this fact, we will miss the real 'folly' and 'scandal' involved in being a follower of Christ in the 20th century. Without a full awareness of the folly, there can be no surrender, and so no holiness. Always there is a danger that we will unconsciously assume Jesus to be a common sense, modern sort of person with a common sense, modern sort of approach to life. When we do that, we abandon christianity. This can happen even if we stay in the Church.

One final gap has to be noticed by clerical readers. Jesus was a layman. He was not a priest or scribe, or in any way an established person. He is called a priest in the New Testament on theological grounds, but socially he was a layman who was not part of the religious establishment. Sometimes we tend to think he was, and so miss the scandalous edge to his behaviour. In other words, the Founder of our religion and the source of our holiness was an unestablished layman from an ordinary family. Catholics brought up on the divinity of Christ (which we believe in) have in practice neglected to accept these implications which are the implications which stem from Christ's genuine humanity (which we also believe in). Our practice of talking about Jesus as 'Our Lord' perhaps contributes to this misunderstanding. 'Our Lord' is a timeless, classless, rather sacerdotal sort of figure, whereas Jesus of Nazareth belonged to a definite time, class, society, which is not that of any of his modern followers. Jesus was a layman in history, whereas 'Our Lord' tends to be all God and not much man.

All this means that if I am to take Jesus as the model of my life I must prepare myself to be changed in ways that may be startling both to myself and other people. Sometimes we fail to try to be holy because we are not really ready for that. We have unconsciously accommodated Christ and his teaching to our accepted standards. But it should be the other way round.* The saints are sent

* As I write this a Society wedding took place in one of our cathedrals. There were 800 guests and it must have cost £4,000. One wonders whether this is a christian celebration in remembrance of Christ (the poor man from Nazareth), or a celebration in honour of Society, with a christian tinge, no more.

53

to show us how taking Jesus Christ seriously means being turned inside out, dropping our accepted standards in favour of those of Jesus. The way to be ready for that is to notice who Jesus was and the culture he belonged to.

The final point in our search is that we are expected to be *disciples* of Jesus Christ. In other words our knowledge of him is not meant to come from an academic study, but precisely in a personal way; from being his disciples in our lives. The way we are meant to know Jesus is by being in his company, as the first disciples were. The Church, the Bible, christian 'tradition' are there to help us be as effective as possible and not wander too far from the truth. But ultimately our knowledge of Jesus Christ is going to be private to each one of us, and to that extent not fully communicable to others. The Lord I have lived with and tried to serve for so long – I know him in a different way than you, the reader, know him. It is the same Lord we serve, but our knowledge of him is personal to each of us. Let us not be side-tracked by the scholars into a search for the 'real Jesus' from documents. The real Jesus is the one you and I have tried to know since we first began to serve him. The exciting thing is that he becomes more real, the more we try to be his disciples. This living figure whom I personally know, is the pivot of holiness for me. He is the standard of my life and becomes more real the more I live up to that standard.

Only if we have submitted to Jesus as his disciples are we ready for the instruction the Church gives us about Christ's divinity and redemptive mission. We ought to know him personally and clear-sightedly first, because that personal 'disciple' knowledge is the foundation of holiness. To put it another way, theological concepts tend to obscure Christ to us if they are not accompanied by personal discipleship of the teacher Jesus. We know this from listening to sermons by preachers who have read books but do not pray. On the other hand, theology is marvellously enlightening if we approach it to clarify an already awakened personal knowledge. We are asked to embrace Christ's teaching not theoretically as an exercise in ideology, but personally because we know and love the man. Holiness grows out of this personal knowledge of Jesus Christ. In other words, we accept him as our master before we accept his words. The personal surrender comes first and is always more important.

*Chapter 9*

# The Standards of Jesus

In their choice of standard for living, disciples of Christ
cannot compromise. If you take 'Christianity' or 'The
Church' as your standard it is perhaps possible to compromise, because these tend to offer standards of shifting
value. They can all too easily be accommodated to worldly
compromise. But Jesus was and is a real person with uncompromising views on society and our relations with
each other and God. Being a disciple of this man was
never easy. He said that for those who elected to follow
him it involved taking up the cross.

Being obedient to Jesus' command to love all men
means sooner or later taking up the cross. In undertaking
the adventure of loving everyone I expose myself to
suffering. A loving, open relationship with someone else
is the best of all human experiences, but it is not cheaply
won. We human beings cannot love each other without
going through experiences which tear us apart but mature
us, experiences like conquering mistrust; learning to for-
give the apparently unforgivable; exposing the private
sectors of our being by letting the defences of human
pride be broken down; learning to be patient and to
conquer anger; having to apologise for humiliating faults;
sharing what we thought was not for sharing; surrendering our independence in the higher interests of love. All
these are risks to be taken and deaths to be undergone. Of

course we go through this at varying levels with varying people. No one is asked to share deeply with everyone he meets. Nevertheless Christ's injunction to his followers to love was clear and uncompromising. When we pull back from being involved in another human being, we are pulling back from Christ himself. Where a vague 'christianity' often allows us to turn our backs on human need and hand responsibility over, Jesus Christ does not. 'When I was hungry, thirsty, naked, in prison . . .' There is no sanctity where there is a withdrawal from this sort of love. The saints go the whole hog here, far beyond the bounds of common sense.

When you do not withdraw from loving another person who needs to be loved, you often find yourself in conflict with the accepted standards of society. Society has a way of building walls and keeping people behind them in manageable groups. Then it sets up unwritten taboos to keep us all in those groups. Society permits us to love within the group but not to break the taboo and love outside it. We are encouraged to love all members of 'us', but not members of 'them'. Without our being made aware of it our love is often narrowly constricted by the powerful phrases 'Nobody does that' or 'It's never been done'. In this way barriers of class, colour, creed and so on are erected even in christian societies. I have known a family in need be refused a bed in a comfortable priests' house on the grounds that it was never done to have lay people sleeping in the presbytery. The clerical taboo among the clergy was stronger than their christian love. The British class system makes it easy to love within taboos but very difficult to love people beyond them. There is a ready acceptance and genuine, warm welcome between members of the same class even when they are strangers to each other. But families of a different social stratum can live beside each other for years and never enter each other's houses. There are unseen barriers between them which allow 'charity' but forbid love to be exchanged. They cannot sit as equals in each other's houses, because the taboo is too strong. Society forces them to be apart. It takes an air raid in wartime or a natural disaster like the house burning down to bring them together.

Jesus Christ came across these taboos in his own day and magnificently disregarded them. His love knew no bounds. As a devout Jew he was not supposed even to speak to the Samaritan woman, but he did. Similarly he ought not to have associated with tax collectors and sinners, but he chose Levi as a follower and mixed with Levi's associates. As a loyal Jew he ought not to have been friendly with the Roman occupying power, but apparently he was, for he cured the Centurion's son when asked to. This sovereign indifference to society's taboos was the reason he was done away with. Much of what he did was against the official interpretation of the Law. He was, therefore, a threat to the established custodians of society and the Jewish Law. So they killed him. It was a death he foresaw and faced for the sake of love. It was the practice side of the doctrine he was always preaching: love all men. In the next generation theological thinkers concluded that his death was 'meant' as the way the Father chose to redeem mankind from sin. They said that Jesus died to redeem man from sin. The sin Christ died to conquer was the sin of lack of love. He conquered it practically in his life and teaching before doing so 'redemptively' in his death. It has entered into theology from the plain facts of Jesus' life.

As a follower of Jesus Christ I am meant in my generation to love in the same way. I have to be sensitive to the needs of everyone around me and I must be prepared to go to the limits. I must be ready to break through any barriers that society may have erected to 'contain' my love within a small group. I should go further and question the existence of those barriers themselves. Implicit, then, in the christian command to love all men is a readiness to criticise the accepted standards of society. Being prepared to stand back and submit the status quo to criticism in the light of the Gospel and then, if necessary, to act unconventionally is one of the tests of sanctity. So many of us do our best to love within the accepted standards but our love is often merely conventional. We do not love 'personally' enough to break the conventions which are less than christian. But the saints do so, not necessarily because they are more intellectual and have made a critique of society, but because they love Jesus Christ so much that his commands mean more than any social convention. They have their eyes fixed on a different aim from that of most of us. Most of us want to do what our 'christian upbringing' or 'the Church' have taught us to conform to. The saints want to do what Jesus wants. And so they are led into mad escapades of 'folly' and 'scandal' like refusing to serve in the German Army when everyone else did (Franz Jägerstätter) or, like Charles de Foucauld going off to live with the Saharan Tuaregs as one of them.

Another way of describing this 'standing apart' from accepted standards and submitting instead to Jesus' standards is to call it renouncing the world. This is a frequent phrase in the New Testament. It does not necessarily mean leaving society and becoming a hermit (though it has meant that for some). It means leaving the accepted standards of the world and adopting the new ones of Jesus Christ. That is, indeed, a flight or 'going out', but it is an exodus in the manner of one's life, not a physical flight. It is a question of the quality of one's life undergoing a flight from worldly standards. It produces a 'pilgrim' state but does not always involve a physical renunciation of life in society. The renunciation is of standards to live by, not of material position. In fact many christian 'pilgrims' are to be found in very worldly surroundings, just as some of those who have physically 'left the world' have not yet renounced its values. Monks and nuns who run schools for the monied classes often conform to worldly standards and accommodate their love to society's taboos, while married men and women of the most 'conventional sort are to be found who have an unbounded love for all men and open their houses to the socially unacceptable.

All this means that following Jesus Christ is not comfortable. He does not want us ever to accept this world without questioning it for love. So the business man has to look to see if business life allows him to be completely christian; and the clergyman has to ask himself whether adopting clerical life in any way prevents him living Christ's Gospel; and the university student must question whether the 'mores' of university life which he slips into so easily are compatible with the Gospel or not. It is not comfortable at all. But it is not so much an intellectual process as a loving one. Holy people bring discomfort upon themselves because they determine to love all men. They love others so much that their actions question society's values. Usually other people supply the intellectual reasons for the questioning. For the saints it all comes from love.

*Chapter 10*

# The Living Christ

So far I have spoken about Jesus as the historical teacher who lived nineteen hundred years ago in Palestine. I have called attention to the real person he was with his cultural characteristics, because I think there is a danger that in our attempt to be holy we may be content merely to embrace christianity as we see it today and forget about Christ. This would be to turn it into a timeless ideology and forget that it is the teaching of a real, and rather shocking, man in history.

But we can say more about Jesus than that he lived in the past and his influence is still with us. Not only is his influence still in this world. He is too. The Resurrection means that Jesus was raised from death and is with us. Jesus of Nazareth is not, therefore, only a figure from history. In some mysterious way, beyond our understanding but not beyond our belief, he is still with us. He promised to be so until the end of time. He keeps his promise. Not a mere memory or influence, not merely living on through his followers in the movement he founded (as Marx or Mahomet does), not a vague spiritual presence, but corporeally with us: the whole Risen Christ with us, invisible, but really present. This is the christian belief. It is an enormous claim. Nevertheless, with a leap of faith we make the claim.

We have a second conviction about Jesus. We believe

not only that he is still present in this world. We also
believe that, by baptism, we are personally linked with
him. In other words, his influence is not just by personal
presence, but by mystical union. We are somehow 'in'
him, and he in us. It is difficult to write about this truth
without breaking into metaphor. Perhaps poetry is the
only way in which the truth can be conveyed. Prose is
not enough. Jesus himself had recourse to poetic symbol.
'I am the Vine; you are the branches,' he said. For St
Paul the truth was expressed in a similar symbol. Jesus
Christ is the Head and we are the members of the same
body. In both these images, the kernel of truth is the
sharing of common life: sap flowing from bush stem to
branches, to leaves, to fruit and back again: blood stream,
nervous system, sinews and muscles all working for the
wellbeing of the one body and controlled organically by
the head. Behind these metaphors is the conviction that
Christ and christians are united intrinsically. This mysticism is not a theological elaboration, but a New Testament doctrine.

To grasp this double truth – the presence of the real
Jesus, his mystical union with us – is to add richness to
the doctrine of abandonment to divine providence mentioned in Chapter 3. There I spoke of the possibility of
walking with God all day by speaking to him: surrendering every moment of the day back to the Creator from
whom it comes. We can now add that this daily abandonment to the Father is done *in Christ*. Our inner union
with Jesus Christ itself is the surrender to the Father we
are striving to make. By ourselves we could not achieve
abandonment to the Father. But we are not by ourselves.
We are baptised into perpetual union with Christ. It is
that permanent union with Jesus which achieves the

required surrender. We do it 'in Christ'. The ticket collector going about his work, the nurse caring for the patients in hospital, because they are baptised christians do all they do in Jesus Christ and for God the Father. They are bathed in the presence and energy of God. You have to use poetry to express this sublime truth:

'I say more: the just man justices;
Keeps grace: that keeps all his goings graces;
Acts in God's eye what in God's eye he is –
Christ – for Christ plays in ten thousand places,
Lovely in limbs, and lovely in eyes not his
To the Father through the features of men's
    faces.'
(G. M. Hopkins)

The danger with poetry is that because it is so beautiful, it lifts us out of the rut of ordinary life. That must not happen in our examination of christian spirituality. Being in Christ, being internally surrendered to the Father, walking with God – this is not a state which transports us away from this world's business. It does not take the christian away from his work or his friends. But it gives a depth which is not there normally. I remember sitting with a group of university lads in a room one evening. We were celebrating Mass and were discussing what each was going to do after leaving university. There was a lot of conventional society rat-race bashing. Then one lad, a quiet, final year biochemist, no great talker, spoke from the corner where he was sitting on the floor. He said he had turned down the possibility of one or two well paid jobs with chemical firms because they were involved in marketing what were, in his opinion, immoral drugs.

He did not know what he was going to do yet. That quiet corner was not the place I had expected a contribution from, but it was the voice of Christ – not just an abstract 'Risen Christ', but the real voice of Jesus of Nazareth, the uncompromising preacher of the Sermon on the Mount. He had taken hold of a very ordinary diffident Scotsman who made no claim to 'christian witness' or 'authentic spirituality' or any fashionable idea. He merely wanted to follow Christ and had worked out what that meant for him. It surprised one or two of those sitting in the group and they tried to water down his decision. He very quietly stood firm. Mass that evening for us all was a true Holy Communion with Jesus Christ, present in our midst.

## Chapter 11

## Conversion to Discipleship

We saw in Part I that we undergo a conversion when it dawns upon us that God is our Father and we are being called to submit our whole lives to him. We may now reflect that this conversion is at the same time a conversion to the standards set up by Jesus, whom the Father sent. Since Jesus is still alive and internally united to us as our strength, this conversion is possible. It is never easy, but it is possible, because invisibly grace is at work in our souls demolishing the compromises which instinctively we put forward, urging us to be conformed to God. 'It's too difficult'; 'nobody goes as far as that – it isn't done'; 'everybody does it – so what's wrong with it?'; 'they go to church every Sunday and *they* do it'; 'theologians are doubtful whether that is strictly required of us'; 'the Church has not yet made a descision on that point'. We are familiar with the voices inside us which water down the stark demands of the Gospel. The saints were familiar with them too, but they faced them and answered them.

Sometimes we never quite face those compromises directly but let them go on murmuring away inside ourselves; and so having never quite faced our compromises, we never quite remove them from our hearts, and settle for an uneasy coexistence of compromise and Gospel. We keep our high principles. We keep our compromises. We are not yet integrated in our souls. Conversion comes when we face Jesus Christ honestly in our hearts, and so face and remove our compromises. Integration then begins. But it is not an immediate process. After the first conversion we have to settle to a lifetime of fidelity to that moment by 'prayer, observance, discipline, thought and action'. It is not the seed which springs up straightaway which produces the harvest, but the seed sown in the rich soil. This wheat takes time to come up, because it first goes down deep. Christian conversion is radical. It goes to the roots.

It is helpful to keep in mind that christian conversion normally takes time. It will prevent us being impatient with the not yet converted, whether they be ourselves or others. With Kierkegaard, again, we have to remind ourselves that we are not yet christians, only travelling towards that state. On our journey we often fall backwards and have to start again. This should not worry us unduly. One of the features of Jesus' teaching is his immense understanding and compassion for people who go on trying but do not always succeed. He did not apparently, warm to people who never failed, 'the Just'. They felt no need for the physician so he left them alone, but the sick the sinners, who admitted they were sinners, were his frequent companions. He loved to be with them. This is comforting news for those of us who are only half converted but still trying.

Christianity in this is remarkable. It demands the highest principles but permits a low performance. It is a religion for those who aim at complete conversion to Christ and his uncompromising ideals but who have not yet been fully converted. It is a religion for sinners trying to be saints. The presence of sinners in christian circles is the guarantee that the spirit of Christ is there. When sinners are treated intolerantly there is an absence of the true Gospel. From time to time in the history of christianity there come reforming movements. Prophets appear with winnowing fans to scatter the chaff and separate off the pure grain. A good test of the sanctity of such zealous reformers is how they treat those who go on trying but do not succeed, those awkward characters who stick out like sore thumbs and spoil the pattern of perfection in the group. Jesus treated repentant sinners and the not yet converted with warm understanding based on hope. They were in fact his disciples! He lived with them and enjoyed their company. He kept on giving them more chances. His reforming followers in history have not always been so tolerant. Many of them have rooted up the tares in the wheatfield at sight and have not waited for the harvest. This intolerant sectarian zeal, so foreign to Jesus Christ, is a wrong turning on the path to holiness. True holiness recognises that the Church is for bad christians as well as for good christians. In many of his novels, Graham Greene spells out Mauriac's saying that 'the sinner is at the heart of Christendom'. As a result he writes genuinely christian novels, in which sanctity is found where the reader would least expect it; among sinners. Understanding the human fact about christian conversion, that it is never complete and frequently in the future, is an essential ingredient of holiness. It is why we have been given the sacrament of confession. In confession we are helped to climb back with dignity to our high ideals by being forgiven our low performances.

## Chapter 12

# Discipleship

As christians we have a loyalty towards our christianity. It figures first in our list of loyalties. It is the one to which we make our other loyalties – family, friends, business, country – defer. We try to make our religion the master ideal which governs all the rest of our life. That is what being a religious person means.

In this chapter let us take a look at the average man's loyalty to christianity and within that one loyalty, distinguish some constituent elements. A person's following out of christianity as a way of life contains three distinct, though intertwined, loyalties. They are his loyal service of the Church (It), his embracing of the christian ideology (Ism) and his devotion to Our Lord Jesus Christ (Him). All three are present in the average christian member of the Church. He or she belongs to it, believes in the christian 'ism', and tries to know and love our Lord. The significant thing is the way in which these three elements are linked in the follower's mind. What looms largest and generates the most loyalty? In other words, which of the three elements is the one which chiefly matters for the christian and makes him tick?

For some christians their closest loyalty is to the Church. They belong to it and have a warm sense of that belonging, both at the local level of parish or religious community, and at the world-wide level of Church. They are concerned about the Church and also proud of it. It means a lot to them that they are members of the local congregation and of the whole Church. For some even the local parish provides the main interest of their lives. Since the Vatican Council this doncern for the Institution has generated a very considerable amount of talk, discussion, writing and conferences among Catholics. It is a tribute to the innate strength of institutionalism in the Catholic Church that we have been so concerned about new structures, new means of communication, new ways of adjusting the relationships between Pope and bishops, bishops and priests, priests and laity. Fresh words like collegiality and co-responsibility have been coined to meet our new concerns. Being a member of the Church has never been such an exciting and / or disturbing thing. For many people it has brought either a new lease of life or a sense of chaos and disaster, because christianity has meant for them primarily belonging to the Church, and changes in the Church have hit them hard and deep. The element of It is being lived to the full.

Another type of christian sees his christianity chiefly in intellectual terms. For him, it is an ideology, an 'ism'. People like this are keenly aware of the changes which are going on in the world today and sensitive to the need for a programme of belief and thought which can direct these changes. Being christians they are aware that christianity claims to be a religion which offers salvation to all the world and hence must tackle the huge problems which face thinking men today. To be true to its nature christianity must not run away from modern problems but face them and look for solutions which are in accordance with the Word of God. As christians we must place ourselves alongside the many men of goodwill who are addressing themselves to mankind's problems and humbly offer our solutions – but only after we have first seen the problems and heeded others' efforts to tackle them. The sort of problems which face mankind today are problems of Ecology, World Population, Justice and Peace, Poverty and the Third World. War, Revolution and Violence, Medicine and the Social Sciences, Capital and Labour, Family Life. We cannot live as human beings and be unaware of the enormous questions which are being posed to mankind in these areas. We are, in fact, caught up in these problems of a culture change ourselves and are only able to afford the luxury of ignoring some because we are in a privileged position in Europe. Others, less fortunate than ourselves (or are they luckier?) have to live faced with these major problems all their lives. What has christianity to say about these modern problems as culture changes before our eyes? As we try to answer that we become conscious of the ideological, 'ism', element in our following of Christ. Part of living out christianity for us must be the search for a christian 'programme' in the modern world, a search to bring the Gospel to bear upon these intractable human questions. Christ taught his followers to look for and then obey the will of the Father. This means that his 20th century followers have to do the same with regard to all the problems of the world today. The will of God concerning these major problems may not be easy to discern, but it exists nevertheless, and we have to try to discover it. We cannot run away from the problems into a merely devotional christianity.

The third element in being a christian is Him. We believe, as outlined in Chapter 10, that Jesus Christ is still alive and present in the modern world, and therefore

70

that being a christian means relating to him personally, submitting our life to him, listening to his demands, being as completely as possible united to him in our hearts. Of the three elements this is the least tangible. It is easier, I think, to become involved in Church problems or in christian ideology problems than in the invisible, perhaps elusive, person of Christ. The first two make sense to modern man and to ourselves. They are measurable and discussible with outsiders. But to talk about submitting oneself to Christ or doing the will of our Lord makes very little sense at the bar of public opinion. But it is just this third element of personal submission to Jesus Christ in christianity which makes for holiness. The saint is the person who moves among the problems of the Church and the world as one deeply committed to Jesus in his heart.

The three elements I have singled out in christianity are not mutually exclusive. On the contrary they are really no more than three aspects of one reality. The true christian keeps them closely together and interrelated, because they *are* just aspects. But there is no doubt which of the elements should be dominant over the other two. The whole point of the Institution is that it is the structure in the world in which Jesus Christ is met and his will proclaimed. The object, after all, of our modern institutional discussions is simply to make Christ's presence in the world better recognised and communicated to others. All other considerations are subordinate to that. If we do not love the Risen Christ, Church problems are nonsense. Similarly the aim of our agonising search for christian solutions to the world's problems is a 'personal' one: to discover what Christ wants for the world. We are not just engaged in an intellectual search.

We are looking for God's will. It may not, of course, be meaningful to talk in those terms to our contemporaries. But it is what we should be saying inside ourselves. It is how we should be seeing the matter, because it is how God sees it!

In 1886 Charles Lwanga and his companions were put to death at Namugongo near modern Kampala, by Kabaka Mwanga of Buganda. They were put to death for refusing to submit to the homosexual demands of the Kabaka, which as officials of his court they were expected to do. There were also political overtones to the killing, Buganda being recently opened up to European influence and Mwanga none too certain of the motives of the newly arrived missionaries who had baptised these men. The heroic death of these young men – they were tied together in bundles and put on a fire – acutely exemplifies the three elements in being a Christian. At one level their death was an institutional victory for the Church. Mwanga died, but the Church grew rapidly. To this day the Church in Uganda makes much of its first martyrs and recognises that their blood was the seed of its growth. At another level the martyrdom was a victory for the christian ethic at a crucial moment when East Africa was being opened up to Europe. It was a striking ideological 'statement' on behalf of the new generation of christian Africans. But the young men themselves did not see it like that. They were aware of those two dimensions, but what made them defy the Kabaka and sustained their courage right up to death was their personal devotion to Jesus Christ. They went ahead with their resistance, singing hymns together on the bonfire, for love of their new Lord. <u>Christianity for them was a matter of devotion to our Lord</u>. But it was a devotion which involved them in an agonising decision about Church and State, not one which enabled them to escape from responsibilities.

All the saints have shown us this truth. They teach us by their lives as well as by their sayings that conversion to christianity is primarily conversion to Christ, though it is simultaneously a conversion which plunges us right into the Church and the world and highlights our responsibilities. As we saw in an earlier chapter, abandonment to the Father may *sound* like escape, but in reality it is engagement. Sophisticated saints like Thomas More have demonstrated this as well as the simple Buganda martyrs. For all the saints, christianity has meant not only membership of the Church but discipleship of Christ. It must be the same for us, as we aspire to holiness.

## Chapter 13

# The Mind of Christ

Conversion leads to prayer. To realise that God is my Father and Jesus Christ is still in some mysterious way alive and linked with me – to *realise* it as a personal fact, not just as theoretically true – is to begin to pray. God is personally interested in me and relates to me. So I begin to relate back to him. My inner personal life now has a new richness. There is a new personality in it, none other than God! Consequently it is the most natural thing in the world to want to spend time in his company and talk with him. When I do this I cross the boundary in my inner consciousness from 'knowing about' God to 'knowing' him. Those who are born and brought up christian first learn as they grow up to 'know about' God and his Son Jesus Christ from the Bible and the teaching of the Church. They grow up with a second hand knowledge of God. They have learnt about him from other people. Something quite different in quality happens, however, when that knowledge about God begins to develop by first hand experience into 'knowing' him. God is now personal, a reality in their life, another Being whom they have to take into account in all their musings. God has, as it were, come alive for them as Father. They now want to take prayer seriously, because it is the response which makes most sense. They want to give themselves personally to this personal God by entering into a relationship with him. Anything less personal than that is insufficient for their newly awakened needs.

The justification for spending time and energy in praying is similar to the justification the mountaineer gave for wanting to climb Everest – 'Because it is there!' God is there. So we pray. We circle round him in adoration and surrender ourselves back to him. It is true that we can walk with God and speak to him all day as we go about our daily work, surrendering to him in the midst of his creation and giving him everything we do from moment to moment. But thank God, we can also do more; and it is this doing more which makes christianity exciting. We can give God more than our daily work. We can give him ourselves. We can give him our time. We can go deep in prayer.

The best gift we have, the gift of self *par excellence*, is time. When I give time to people I give them myself. It is, most preciously, *me*. That is why I guard it jealously and hate to waste it. But I waste it with my friends! That is how I go deep with them – by spending time with them. So it is with God in prayer. When we want to give ourselves genuinely to God we surrender him our time by devoting large portions of it to him in prayer. That is the language of love: waste! Lovers waste time with each other in a gloriously spendthrift manner. They do not look for any further justification for doing so than that it is good to do it. They are incapable of not doing it. Because they are in love they are impelled to be with each other. It is, I suggest, not fanciful, but the logic of love, the logic of the saints, to justify prayer in the same way. Prayer is a waste of our time, given as generously as possible to God: our gift of self.

Justifications for devoting time to prayer along any other lines are essentially insufficient. Prayer is an opportunity to consider salvation in depth; it is a pause for refreshment between bouts of christian activity; it is a charging of batteries, recouping of energies. These reasons for praying speak in terms of getting something out of prayer. But just because prayer is a personal relationship they fall short of the mark. You do not enter into a relationship with another person with your mind on what benefits will accrue to you. To do so would be to abuse the relationship and never really 'connect'. It is the same with God. We go to pray, to adore, to be with God, because he is God and we are his children. We give him our time, and there is no other reason needed to justify that than to say he is our Father. In all this we are but following in the footsteps of Jesus himself who was a spendthrift of time in regard to prayer. Though his days were busy with people, he went off at nights to pray. Communing with the Father was so important to him that he gave up sleep for it. He did not spend nights in prayer in order to obtain something spiritual for himself or his mission. He went just to be with his Father.

The more we are converted to the mind of Christ the more we will be drawn to give time to be with God in prayer. This is not easy in an urban civilisation where life runs along at a rattling pace and there are few natural pauses in the day or week. But I suspect it was never easy to find time to give to prayer. Probably we deceive ourselves with the idea that in earlier, rural, civilisations there was time for prayer. I think it has always been difficult to find. There has, probably always been an initial sacrifice asked before our prayer becomes serious. That is certainly so today.

Experience shows that nobody becomes a person of prayer without giving up, quite decisively, something which is quite dear to him. This can be reading, watching television, listening to the radio, chatting and gossiping, sleep. All of them good things, and that is the point. We are not required merely to give up bad things in order to pray. We are asked to squeeze out some of the quite useful things in our life if we wish to enter deeply into the field of prayer. They are good things; but in christian discipleship very often the good is discovered to be the enemy of the best. Another way of putting this is to say that God asks us to make a sacrifice as he draws us fully into the intimacy of prayer. He wants us to 'show willing' before he gives his graces. The last-named sacrifice on the list, sleep, is a case in point. Many have found that the invitation to go deep in prayer was at the same time an invitation to give up sleep for it. This is because we have little time to spare between breakfast and bedtime in a busy life, but there is time to give between bedtime and breakfast. It is also because there is something specially valuable in the hours of night for prayer. The saints have been great vigil makers. In the silence of the night and in the early morning they have found God.

The prayer I am referring to is personal prayer; that is, the prayer of relating personally to God. You cross a Rubicon when you move from thinking about God (meditation) to talking to God (prayer). It is the difference between manipulating concepts about God and opening out towards him beyond concepts and words. In meditation we are in charge, drawing up our thoughts, arranging our conclusions and making resolutions. It is a necessary and fruitful thing for christians to do, but it is not yet prayer. It is not prayer because when we do it, we are only talking to ourselves about God. In other words, it is an exploration into knowing about God. But when you pray you stop talking to yourself and talk to God. You stop trying to 'know about' and begin to 'know'. Immediately you find you are no longer in charge. You have

77

entered into a relationship with another Being, and that other Being is now dominant. All relationships involve this act of letting go and no longer being in full control – otherwise there is no relationship; you have to deliver yourself over at least partially to the other person before the relationship becomes two-way. But when the other person in the relationship is God, the unpredictable, unknowable Creator of the universe, then it is very much a question of man being no longer in control of things. You give yourself to God and he quite simply takes over. It is an awesome happening.

When this takes place we often want to scuttle back to the safe side of the Rubicon, and we go back to meditation. We feel more secure just thinking about God and drawing our conclusions. But if we make an act of trust in God's merciful purpose and lovingly abandon ourselves to him, great things are in store for us. What is in store for us is nothing less than a personal relationship with God! Once we let go inside ourselves, cease to try to use words and launch out on the uncharted seas of silent communion God will draw us into a rich adventure of partnership with him. Partnership, however, is not a good word to describe what eventually happens. It is too 'external'. What happens, happens deep down inside us. We are drawn into such intimate communion with God inside ourselves that one day we seem to merge with the Godhead, while still remaining sinful humans. Something in the depth of our personalities 'let's go' and we 'become' God. Jesus said 'I and the Father are one'. For him it had a special meaning not open to us. But in prayer we experience something like it. It is, perhaps, what St Paul meant by being given the mind of Christ. In Christ, in prayer, we become one with the Father. It is the fulfilment of our baptism.

## Chapter 14

# Abba Father and the Cloud of Unknowing

There is an old story of two prisoners sharing a cell because of overcrowding in the prison, who, to while away the long hours of boredom together, used to swap funny stories. After a time they knew all the jokes by heart so instead of narrating the jokes they used to say them by numbers. 'Number five' – this would produce laughter. 'Yes, and what about number seventeen?' More laughter would follow.

This story illustrates how prayer develops once we have crossed the Rubicon from knowing about God to knowing him. At first we have to use plenty of narrative to prepare ourselves for love. Love does not start from ignorance, but needs to be fed with ideas. But the more we continue in prayer, the more we are familiar with God and know more about him, so the less is narrative necessary. We find that we have heard all about God's love and Christ's Redemption before and are in a hurry in prayer to get to the time when we do the loving. So we skip lengthy narrative. A word or two suffices. Rather than an imaginative assembling of Gospel data in our minds we prefer one word: 'Gethsemane!' 'Tabor!' The single word evokes all that we want to say; it is not necessary – but distracting – to go through the whole story. God and ourselves have reached that stage of familiarity which the prisoners sharing the cell had reached. There is now a private one word code between us. We use it to evoke and share love. With a single word love wells up and brims over in our hearts.

There is a long tradition in christian spirituality for using short words and phrases in prayer. The Jesus Prayer, so much loved by eastern christians, has a considerable practice and literature which has gathered round it down the ages. It is one of the great spiritual Ways in christian tradition. It is still much in use and found to be invaluable. In the West, too, short phrases and words have been recognised as an authentic way for contemplative prayer. The 14th century *Cloud of Unknowing* gives this advice to the man who has been drawn into the practice of simple prayer:

'If thou desirest to have this (naked intent unto God) lapped and folded in one word, so that thou mayest have better hold thereupon, take thee but a little word of one syllable, for so it is better than of two; for the shorter the word, the better it accordeth with the work of the spirit. And such a word is this word GOD or this word LOVE.' (Ch. 7)

and again in a later chapter:

'And therefore must we pray in the height and the depth, in the length and the breadth of our spirit. And that not in many words, but in a little word of one syllable. And what shall this word be? Surely such a word as is best suited to the property of prayer.' (Ch. 39)

We surely find echoes of this in the New Testament where the work of the Holy Spirit is described by St Paul. 'When we cannot choose words in order to pray properly, the Spirit himself expresses our plea in a way that could never be put into words' (Rom. 8:26). Significantly the prayer which the Holy Spirit is said to be making in our hearts all the time is not a lengthy oration but either wordless or the single word aspiration 'Abba!' 'The Spirit you received is not the spirit of slaves bringing fear into your lives again; it is the spirit of sons, and it makes us cry out, Abba Father!' (Rom. 8:15). This one word 'Abba!' addressed to the Father has helped many christians in prayer. Like the holy name 'Jesus', it has proved a valuable vehicle for deep prayer. Consecrated short words like 'Jesus' and 'Abba' are rich evocations of the whole of God's relations with us and consequently are ideal for the purpose of simple prayer. We need do no more than say them slowly with plenty of silences in between. In those silences we place the love which is in our hearts.

Silence is the communication of love. When strangers meet they have to keep talking to each other. Between strangers silence is a breakdown in communication. Only by using plenty of words can they get anything across to each other. Between friends it is different. Friends can keep silent with each other without feeling threatened; because it is one of the ways they communicate. They can spend time in each other's company and emerge with mutual understanding, though they may not have said much in the way of words. Among friends both words and the silences in between have meaning. This is how prayer between the baptised christian and God his Father proceeds. At first there have to be many words and concepts because intimacy has not yet been established between the soul and God. But once launched on the way of prayer, the way of abandonment to the Father, words become less necessary or desirable and silence takes over. This silence goes deeper and deeper, fuller and fuller of mysterious sharing, as love grows. The pool of our souls brims over with love. All descriptions of this loving silence in prayer and what goes on in it are inevitably inadequate, but one of the least inadequate was given by Jean Louis Chaffengeon. Jean Louis was the old man in Ars who spent his days at the back of the church. When the Curé asked him what he did all day, Jean Louis replied, 'I look at him. He looks at me.' This marvellously simple description puts into words what many people have experienced when they have been drawn deep in silent prayer.

The final stage in any human relationship is the moment when words become an actual hindrance to communication. They get in the way because they cannot express what one wants to express. Only silence can do that. It is not an empty silence, but a silence charged with rich meaning like a thundercloud heavy with rain. We reach these situations with people who move us deeply. They make us speechless with anger, speechless with wonder and love. We can't use words. There aren't any for our purpose. So we keep silence, the silence of intense meaning, the silence of 'atmosphere' between two people. So it is in prayer. There come moments when even the monosyllables of love or the name of God break down and we are content to stay still and be drawn into God in deep, atmospheric silence. These are moments of holy communion in Christ with the eternal Godhead. We seem to be drawn even beyond 'looking at' God, because we are now in him and he in us. It is a question of union. Deep down inside us, in that ground of our being spoken of by the mystics, our separateness gives way, and we become one with God.

When people read about this kind of prayer they instinctively feel that such depths are not for them. It somehow seems incompatible with family life and the business of everyday living. They feel safer sticking to 'saying their prayers' and would not like to risk becoming involved in anything deeper. And yet this day to day union with God is implicit in every christian's baptism and is meant for all, not just a select few. One of the features, moreover, of christianity in this generation is that that feeling of diffidence about prayer is fading away. All over the world christians of differing denominations and ages are discovering silent, wordless prayer. In some cases it has been an interest in eastern religions which has led them to rediscover the contemplative way in christianity. In other cases it has been something in christianity itself, like group prayer or night vigils. Be the point of discovery christian or non-christian, sacred or secular, the fact is that in discovering a simple silent form of prayer christians are discovering something precious in their own heritage, not a foreign importation.

Simple prayer is implicit in every christian's baptism. Baptism joins us to God's family. We now can, by grace, call Christ our brother, God our Father. We are baptised *into* the divine family of Father, Son and Holy Spirit, not linked to it externally. The linking agent is within each of us, the Holy Spirit, who dwells in the depths of our hearts. The work of the Spirit is precisely to unite us to God while still living ordinary secular lives in this world. He does this, as we have already noted, by *prayer*. In the depths of each of our hearts he prays 'Abba!'. Because we are now in grace, 'in the family' and not outside it (which is where by nature we ought to be), we should treat God 'familiarly'. Treating God familiarly is another name for the simple prayer I have been describing. There is no need any longer for formality or distance with the Father. It is against our privileged baptismal state to treat God distantly. The Spirit in us is urging us to be familiar and simple. Very reverently, with the awe that comes from wonder and love, we are led by the Spirit to say 'Abba!'. All christians are offered that. Not a select band of chosen souls, carefully groomed by monastic asceticism, but every baptised christian; the ticket collector, the nurse, the politician, the priest – all are drawn forward into simple, wordless prayer. Once drawn, they need no argument to convince them of its appropriateness for them. They know they have come into their own.

A number of discoveries, each to do with sanctity in the modern world, emerge from the practice of simple prayer by everyday christians. The first is that prayer is essentially a service and only secondarily an experience. We pray in order to give, not in order to get. It is of course true that we derive enormous benefits from contemplative prayer. It deepens us and settles us in the pilgrim way. But we will not pray contemplatively if we enter upon it with the desire for experience uppermost in our minds. To approach prayer in terms of spiritual experience is to miss the point that it is a relationship with God, not a personal, subjective event. In prayer we go out to the other who is God. Although this happens in the depths of our being, it is not a turning in upon ourselves, but a being turned inside out by God – an exodus. Many who approach prayer in search of spiritual experience only meet themselves at greater depth. This is not the same as meeting God. It is the difference between meditation and prayer, between making conclusions for oneself *about* God and talking *to* God. The point of difference is whether we want to serve God and others or just ourselves: the point of *service*.

A second discovery which we make when we go deep in prayer has already been mentioned. We experience an increasing sense of being baffled. We feel that we can no longer make any statements about God which are helpful or accurate. God looms larger than ever in our minds, so large that we realise that he is too big and incomprehensible for us to understand. We cannot put God into words. I will not dwell on this point because already in this book we have come to it more than once. It is the point made in Chapter 5 that God is too big for human concepts; that before God man cannot proceed with his usual practice of attempting to control by words; that human statements about God in view of our experience in prayer are seen to be hopelessly anthropomorphic; that between the human mind and God is the cloud of unknowing. But the marvellous thing is that through all this experience of bafflement we can continue to contact God in a hidden way with love and experience union with him. Although thoughts and concepts about God have broken down and the mind finds itself at a standstill, somehow the heart is still very active. We are compelled to go on loving God, and so, in some mysterious way, our love reaches through the cloud of unknowing, and touches God the other side. The book of that name says: 'By love may he be gotten and holden, but by thought never'. Many ordinary christians have experienced that without being able to put it into words.*

We do not experience the cloud of unknowing only in personal private prayer. Perhaps our supreme experience of it is at Mass when we share together what can never be fully comprehended by men. Dick Williams has put it well:

* Older Catholics have for years sung before the Blessed Sacrament: *'Quia te contemplans totum deficit'* – a beautifully succinct description of this truth.

'Before I come to Communion today I think about the bread and wine.

I know that there are some things which are beyond the power of words to express. Surely that is why He took bread, and broke and gave it!

Words can change their meaning, and there is the constant need for retranslation.

But with this action Christ spoke to men of every tongue and in all ages.'
                                        (*God Thoughts*. p. 65)

As a priest I have experienced the ineffability of our saving God at many Masses in widely differing situations. As a student at a papal Mass in St Peter's when the huge jostling congregation was silenced by the silver trumpets at the consecration; in the Roman catacombs early in the morning in whispers; with university students in a room. Once a group of us in discussion spent an evening trying to express our thoughts and ideals about poverty. It was a discussion over a gospel passage at Mass. We discussed hard but ran into muddles and failed to find the right words and any agreement. But then in breaking the Bread and sharing the Wine in the room together we disovered the meaning we were looking for in the silent, broken Body and Blood of Our Lord. We were gathered together and reached agreement in a holy communion which transcended words.

The reader will have his own experiences of the word-lessness of God's love. God gives this grace to all of us from time to time. These moments when we are drawn beyond human words are given to us as glimpses of the sanctity we have not yet attained. They beckon us forward to that promised fulfilment in God, the condition of complete simplicity costing not less than everything.

## Part Three

## SPIRIT

## Chapter 15

# Wind and Fire

Jesus Christ lingers on in this world not merely as a memory kept alive by his followers, nor merely through the astonishing impact he made on history, but as a real personal presence. Christians believe that this presence of Jesus in the world is not only real (though mysterious and invisible) but also internal to his followers. We believe that in some mysterious way we are united internally to the Risen Jesus Christ. The metaphor Jesus used to describe this fact was that of the Vine and the branches. Speaking in another idiom at the Last Supper, but about the same fact, he promised to send the Holy Spirit. This Spirit, he said, would be sent by the Father and him, and would come upon his followers and live within them. The Spirit would be the inner energy by which they lived the life of that 'new creation' which he, Jesus, had brought about among mankind. The Spirit would, therefore, be a spirit of truth, guiding their minds to deeper and fuller understanding of the insights taught by him; and also a spirit of love inflaming their hearts with the courage and love to live according to those new truths. The expected Spirit from God was the new heart of flesh which the prophet Ezekiel had foretold would be given to the Jews at the time of the Messiah, in place of their all too hard hearts of stone. So they welcomed the Spirit's arrival with enthusiasm.

When the Spirit came he came with wind and fire. The wind blew round the house, the fire burnt upon each of the apostles' heads. It was a great external show of the power of God. It was followed by another external miracle: the understanding of what the apostles were preaching by the huge crowd of people who all spoke different languages. These miracles of Pentecost have been celebrated ever since by the Church. The very spectacular-ness of the outward happenings of Pentecost, however, could divert attention from the inner happenings. What happened inwardly at Pentecost, and what happens inwardly now in Christ's followers, is the important thing. The Holy Spirit, as his name implies, is given to us inside ourselves. His love is 'poured into our hearts', in St Paul's fine phrase. He is the new sacred inner spirit, the heart of flesh instead of the heart of stone, which enables us to live as dedicated followers of Christ in the secular world. In other words, the Holy Spirit is a spirit of conversion and daily renewal within us. He is the Spirit of christian holiness. In yielding to his promptings we become holy.

It is helpful to remember about the wind and the fire. We have within ourselves, since baptism, a powerful force which like a wind blows all the cobwebs of sin and selfishness away and which burns down all the barriers we erect against living out our christianity generously. It is worth recalling that in modern life wind and fire are two of the things we take out insurance policies against! Perhaps in our christian lives we have grown accustomed to insuring against the action of the Holy Spirit? Perhaps we pay an annual premium of controlled christian practice (nothing against common sense or social convention, or anything that would be too shocking, but a steady practice of our religion) so as not to have to be exposed to the wind and fire of the Holy Spirit. The Holy Spirit can be such a gale force in the life of a christian that we instinctively hide behind barriers to avoid being caught. The saints are there, however, as awkward reminders that some do not hide away from the Spirit of God, but allow him full play in their lives. They expose themselves to the wind and the fire and trust God enough to yield to him. This is another version of that internal abandonment to the Father which we have been examining. The Holy Spirit is the divine force within us which enables us in all the vicissitudes of life to surrender to God completely. He says 'Abba' deep within us and so hands the control of our lives over to God. It is a total conversion. Though it often starts with an instantaneous happening, this conversion is a lifetime's process. It works itself out through stops and starts, falls and recoveries, until we finally belong wholly to the Father.

## Chapter 16

# The Problem of Narcissus

Because the Holy Spirit is the spirit of love, he is the spirit of immediacy. Love is immediate. It ends at people, not purely subjective intermediaries. Today, it is fatally easy to become involved in subjective intermediaries instead of becoming involved in people. Twentieth-century man is self-analytical and result-orientated. We have perfected the instruments of psychological and social analysis beyond the dreams of our fathers, so that now we are able to evaluate the basic human actions of knowing, loving, relating to people in impressive scientific terms. We do this in order to improve our relationships. We are result-orientated and use analysis to get better results. We live in a world of business surveys, socio-logical research, feedback and computerised evaluation, and it is only to be expected that this spirit should spill over into the field of human relationships. Thus we can examine two people relating to each other and express scientifically how they are doing it. Is one projecting his unconscious needs upon the other? Is there a transference of guilt going on? Is the love between them mature or immature, real or hung up on adolescent phantasies? What is the hidden agenda of the encounter? How much does each know the subconscious dynamic that is going on between them and how is he handling the knowledge that he has? The social sciences deal in concepts like this. Social workers are trained to be able to analyse and evaluate their own relationships and those of other people with more scientific awareness than ever before. Where our ancestors worked with more or less instinctive perception, the modern social worker works with analytical science. It is all a marvellous step forward in man's understanding of himself and his powers of knowing and loving.

The danger, however, is the danger of Narcissus. It is the danger that all the expertise in analysis and evaluation will, in the hands of the inexpert, lead to no real relationships at all, but only a gigantic illusion of relating which covers an increasing turning in on self. The tools of social analysis are dangerous weapons. If I have been given an expertise in analysing my relationships the temptation is very strong to be using this expertise all the time. The result is that instead of relating (i.e. actually knowing and loving the person I am meeting) I may spend the time evaluating my relationship – not the same thing at all. Not the same thing, because knowing and loving someone else means looking at *him* (not me), reacting to *him* (not me), becoming involved in *him* (not me). It is one thing to become absorbed in a person and his problems; it is another, separate, thing to become absorbed in oneself attempting to be absorbed in another person. The two actions cannot be combined simultaneously. There is a place for both. One is immediate and direct, the other is analytical and indirect. More important, one is personal, the other is impersonal. Clearly they are intimately connected but they are two distinct operations. What is important is to see that, though analysis of my relationship with people can be helpful if severely controlled,

I am here in this world to know, love and care for other people, not just myself. It is more important to plunge into caring for other people and risk making all sorts of psychological mistakes than to hesitate on the brink, forever calling a halt in order to evaluate where one has got to in a relationship and to correct one's handling of the situation. Knowing and loving people is like riding a bicycle. Too much looking down to see how one is doing and whether the machinery is working properly means that one will lose balance and fall off. The thing to do is to look where one wants to go and then go! It is better to go hard on a faulty bike than to sit looking at oneself on a perfect one.

I have stressed the narcissistic danger because it is a prevalent one today and all the more insidious because it comes from an excess of zeal, not from selfishness. It is those who get involved in caring for other people who run the risk of getting depersonalised by the psychological and sociological tools of the trade. There are social workers who are so busy analysing their relationships with their clients that their clients' needs go unregarded. You can see them assessing the situation according to the text books as they talk to you. You guess that what keeps them going is some cerebral project concerned with people's social needs rather than plain love from the heart. In the same way there are middle-class married couples whose analysis of their failing marriage is so expert and scientific that it is very difficult for them to stop looking at themselves and begin to love each other. Two knowledgeable Narcissi living in separate boxes and killing with science each approach from the other. They are off balance because they look at the bicycle so much that they forget to ride.

Martin Buber summed up this danger in an unforgettable story.

'When I was eleven years of age, spending the summer on my grandparents' estate, I used, as often as I could do it unobserved, to steal into the stable and gently stroke the neck of my darling, a broad dapple-grey horse. It was not a casual delight but a great, certainly friendly, but also deeply stirring happening. If I am to explain it now, beginning from the still very fresh memory of my hand, I must say that what I experienced in touch with the animal was the Other, the immense otherness of the Other, which, however, did not remain strange like the otherness of the ox and the ram, but rather let me draw near and touch it. When I stroked the mighty mane, sometimes marvellously smooth-combed, at other times just as astonishingly wild, and felt the life beneath my hand, it was as though the element of vitality itself bordered on my skin, something that was not I, was certainly not akin to me, palpably the other, not just another, really the Other itself; and yet it let me approach, confided itself to me, placed itself elementally in the relation of Thou and Thou with me. The horse, even when I had not begun by pouring oats for him into the manger, very gently raised his massive head, ears flicking, then snorted – quietly as a conspirator gives a signal meant to be recognisable only by his fellow-conspirator; and I was approved. But once – I do not know what came over the child, at any rate it was childlike enough – it struck me about the stroking, what fun it gave me, and suddenly I became conscious of my hand. The game went on as before, but something had changed, it was no longer the same thing. And the next day, after giving him a rich feed, when I stroked my friend's head he did not raise his head.'

(*Between Man and Man*, pp. 41–2.)

You cannot think your way out of the problem of Narcissus. You can only love your way out of it. It is *thinking* which creates the problem. Scientific analysis and conceptualisation produce the difficulty and so the more you try to think about it the more you fall into the trap. If I sit down and think about the relationship I have with another and how it has gone wrong, I can become paralysed into inaction and so, unintentionally, prolong the faulty relationship. The only way out is to place my conceptual knowledge of the relationship firmly in the background and, fixing my eyes directly upon the other person, determine to care for him. In this way I will forget myself and become involved in his cares and needs. Immediately I will have left the realm of theoretical abstraction and entered that of concrete persons. It is the difference between loving philanthropy and loving people, between setting up projects for the under-privileged and helping real persons, between being absorbed in interpersonal relationships and actually knowing people. In this we are drawn forward by the Holy Spirit. He helps us to break through the web of narcissistic analysis and meet real people whom we can love and who love us. This gift of immediacy in our dealings with people is a gift of the Spirit, because it is the gift of love. By this gift the Spirit exposes us, sometimes brutally, to concrete people who both love us and hate us, console us and hurt us. Once exposed like this, we do not want to go back to impersonal analysis. The exposure turns us away from analysis which tends to be narrowing, towards involvement in real people which is expanding. Those who give themselves over to this Spirit of love find themselves increasingly given over to other people in all their concreteness. In this way they find themselves turned outward from themselves and, having done so, find fulfilment. The fulfilment which Christ brought us was not, therefore, so much one which replenishes our minds with knowledge as one which replenishes our hearts with love.

## Chapter 17

# Narcissus at Prayer

One of George Herbert's hymns has this stanza:

> 'A man may look on glass.
> On it may stay his eye;
> Or, if it pleaseth, through it pass,
> And then the heaven espy.'

It is the poet's way of expressing the problem outlined in the last chapter. We saw that self-analysis, though clearly useful in its place, becomes an obstacle to loving people concretely when elevated beyond its station. This is still more true in prayer than in social work. The danger of self-regard and self-analysis in prayer is great. When a man has become interested in prayer, spoken to people about it, compared his method with those of others, read a book or two on the subject, the danger is that he may go back and never pray well again. The reason would be that he had become so absorbed in 'prayer' that he was no longer absorbed in God. But true prayer is looking at God as directly as possible, not looking at self looking at God. Jean Louis Chaffengeon spent his days looking at God and letting God look at him. He was a man of true prayer who knew God and was, we guess, sublimely ignorant about 'prayer'.

The problem, then, in approaching prayer is the same problem as in approaching one's relationships. We have to love our way through to God himself and not dwell in the intermediaries. Prayer is the window we use to look on God, and the whole point of a window is that you do not look *at* it, but through it. There is a way of standing at a window and looking at the glass, not the view. You can even manoeuvre yourself so as to see your own reflection in the window. But neither of those actions is what the window is for. The window is for looking out of at the view. If we 'stay our eye' on the glass or shape of the window we have missed the point, and missed the chance to 'heaven espy'.*

There is need to consider this today, because of the current revival of interest in prayer. The 'God is dead' phase in christianity has given way to a 'prayer is alive' phase. Many christians of all denominations are showing a genuine interest in prayer, in old and new forms. At one end of the spectrum people are rediscovering the value of wordless contemplation, sometimes from non-christian eastern sources. At the other end is the rapid growth of group prayer and pentecostal prayer. Prayer, after having been decisively 'out', is now very much 'in'. All this is very healthy as long as we remember the lesson of the window (which is the same lesson as that of Buber's horse). The Spirit will lead us towards real, prayerful contact with God, in old and new ways, if we concentrate on God, not on 'prayer'. He is drawing us into encounter with God, into being absorbed in the Father by forgetting

* A friend, reading this, pointed out that the purpose of a window is not only for looking out of, but for letting light in. This is the most important point of all, applied to prayer.

ourselves. Let us be enthusiastic about God in a joyful 'Abba', and pray the way we are inspired without inhibitions. This is not quite the same as being enthusiastic about prayer, pentecostalism, contemplation, liturgy, celebration, or any of those other 'windows' between us and God.

Narcissus when he prays does perhaps more harm than Narcissus among people. In the Catholic Church, which is now in a remarkably self-evaluating phase after the Vatican Council, there is a need to stress the danger of this narcissism, so that we do not get bogged down in the pursuit of Liturgical Experience or Forms of Prayer instead of the pursuit of God. Among other things, the pursuit of means in prayer instead of the End who is God is a way of postponing the meeting with God. Instinctively we fear that; so we dally as long as we can with means and methods.

How will we be delivered from this search for religious experience in prayer rather than God? One way is to remind ourselves constantly that prayer is primarily a service of God and only secondarily an experience. In prayer we surrender to God, give him our whole lives, lay ourselves open before him, expose ourselves to him to use as he wishes. Prayer, in other words, is the proper expression of our service of God, our desire to give him everything and 'not to count the cost'. It is an action of giving. It is, therefore, a misunderstanding to approach prayer in an attitude of 'getting', of looking for a prayerful experience. It is indeed true that God our Father who loves us gives us many benefits from prayer and these include rich experiences *in* prayer. But it is missing the point to approach prayer primarily with a view to what we get out of it. The point of prayer is adoration and love.

In neither of these is 'receiving' or 'experience' the main motivation. We are back to the eleven-year-old Martin Buber and the distinct change which came over his game when he began to care more for stroking the horse than for the horse.

In teaching us to pray the Holy Spirit finally takes the matter out of our hands and educates us by drawing us forward willy-nilly into the aridities of the desert. Prayer ceases for us to be an enjoyable experience or even to have a ready meaning. Self-satisfaction and security in our life of prayer fade away like the mist. We are left without any of the old certainties or consolations. We are in the desert. This can be a bewildering and disillusioning experience, especially for those who have embraced the prayer life with enthusiasm. To have started out so well and undergone new deep experiences in prayer – and then find the experiences have evaporated, leaving only a dull boredom. This is disillusioning to say the least. Usually we feel, when this happens, that something has gone wrong and that it is our fault we no longer get anything out of prayer. We anxiously interpret this as no longer pleasing God. But this experience happens most regularly to those who have committed no great fault in their lives and who have tried hard in prayer. It is, in fact, an almost universal experience. Everyone who sets himself to pray in earnest sooner or later reaches this stage of aridity and boredom. It is not a sign of something 'going wrong' in prayer. If we interpret it rightly we can discern the Spirit at work in this experience of desert.

The experience of the desert in prayer does not happen by accident. In God's plan it is how we are taught to pray for God's sake and not for our own sake. Dryness in prayer (provided it is not caused by our own lack of trying*) is sent by God to teach us to look through the window out upon the view. God makes looking at the window distasteful in order to make us look through it for the view. If we, then, persevere through boredom and bewilderment and carry on in faithfulness to the Father, our motivation about prayer is purified. We cannot any longer be said to be praying for what we get out of it, since that experience has ceased. We are now praying for God's sake, giving ourselves over to him in naked adoration because he is God, not because it is an enjoyable spiritual experience. We are now beginning to serve God for his own mysterious self, not for his gifts of consolation. We have been turned inside out in our approach to prayer. We no longer love 'prayer' (which is dry and unappealing) but God. Narcissus has been killed, and it was the desert 'non-experience' which did it. We begin to see, behind the not very pleasant, dull happenings of our prayer life, the medicinal working of the Holy Spirit. Wind and fire are not always exciting or spectacular. Sometimes they are slow instruments of purification, seen by few people but effecting much good.

In this paradoxically dull way the Holy Spirit draws us forward on the road to holiness. It is a road that leads us through the death of self-reliance and self-satisfaction to deep reliance on God. The Holy Spirit teaches us the lesson enunciated by Jesus that we have to lose our life in order to save it. We have to lose our confidence in ourselves as persons of prayer before we really meet God in prayer. Until we have been through the desert experience and proved that we can endure it, our prayer is inevitably mixed with spiritual self-satisfaction. Only in

* Sometimes it is helpful to talk this particular point over with a wise friend or 'director'. No one is a good judge of his own case.

101

the desert do we bump up against God nakedly and adore him without intermediaries. Self-satisfaction is stripped away; we forget self; and adore! We realise that God is God and duly acknowledge it. This is the gift of immediacy.

*Chapter 18*

# Letting Go of Possessions

In the first chapter of the Book of Job, Job is tested concerning his abandonment to God. Being a rich man with a prosperous family around him and all the wealth he could desire, it could well be that his service of God is tinged with cupboard love. Perhaps he keeps in with God in order to preserve his prosperity and station in life? It is relatively easy for Job to be God-fearing since he loses nothing thereby. It could be that he loves his prosperity first and foremost and God only comes second. How genuine, in fact, is Job's religious adherence to God? These are Satan's questions, and Satan is allowed by God to test him in a series of natural disasters: Job loses everything he had – cattle, sheep, camels servants, his own sons and daughters, his house – all are taken from him. He is left entirely without possessions in total misfortune, with nothing, and nobody, to call his own except a nagging wife, on his dunghill. The question now is whether Job without possessions is as God-fearing as the former rich and prosperous Job. Is he an all-weather friend of God, or merely a fair-weather friend? Does he love God unconditionally, with no strings attached to his devotion? Or were his possessions part of the conditions he laid down for serving God? Satan gets his answer. The poor, dispossessed Job is as God-fearing as he formerly was when rich. He is as admirably 'abandoned' in his poverty

as he was in his prosperity. Possessions have not come
between him and God.

> 'Naked I came from my mother's womb,
> naked I shall return.
> Yahweh gave, Yahweh has taken back.
> Blessed be the name of Yahweh.'

We may think the character of Job in that chapter is a
bit priggish. There is, however, nothing priggish about
Jesus Christ. His message for his followers concerning
possessions was a vigorous one. He turned our attention
to the flowers in the field and the birds in the air and told
us to be like them. A joyful freedom, a happy lack of
anxiety over the goods of this world, was to be the mark
of his followers. Jesus clearly knew that the root obstacle
to man's surrender to the Father is the deep-seated man of
property (Forsyte) in us all. Because we like to be *in
possession*, we find it hard to give everything to God. This
bourgeois in us is both complacent and anxious – complacent because we say: This property is mine and will
remain mine; anxious because we also say: It's mine,
don't take it from me. Most of us have this spirit. If we
are well off it shows rather ostentatiously: the com-
placency can afford to parade itself a bit. But poor people
are Forsytes too, and can be possessive over the small
things which they own. Anxiety and envy are the ways in
which the root obstacle shows in their case. In our
prosperity-chasing, capitalist society this root obstacle is
by no means hidden. Its roots are indeed deep within all
of us, but the flowers romp gloriously for everyone to
see. The Sunday paper colour supplements are weekly
indicators to the foliage. They are based on the assump-

tion that all men are greedy and will buy expensive things if their greed is appealed to.

Jesus made a direct challenge to this way of life. His life, his words, his death were totally free of the possessive spirit. He was independent of material things like a house, a job, food, sleep and comfort. He was also, deeper down, independent of those intangible things which men cling to and without which they feel insecure: other people's esteem encouragement, approval. A normal human being needs all these things, both the material things to keep his body going, and the immaterial things to give him a place in society, an 'identity' among men. We cannot, in fact, live without them except for short periods. They are human needs. They were human needs for Jesus too. Like any other human being he could not live without food and drink, or a human identity. But it is one thing to have needs and be a slave to them, and quite another to have needs and be master of them. Jesus showed that he was master of his life by being independent of his needs. 'Foxes have holes and the birds of the air have nests, but the Son of Man has nowhere to lay his head.' He did not deny that the things of this world like food, drink, clothing, somewhere to live, are good things. He was no puritan. But he was no hedonist either, and in his life and teaching he taught men how to live with the good things of this world by being detached from them; non-possessive and poor in spirit. Independence from riches is the message of the Sermon on the Mount. This is only achieved by the way of poverty of spirit. It is the way to true freedom. Until we make ourselves unpossessive about our property we are slaves to it. Our property owns us, instead of the other way round. Poverty of spirit is the way which leads to true freedom, an inner freedom from anxiety over our possessions, the freedom which comes when we have 'let go' inside ourselves.

Jesus presents this challenge to his followers and sends his Spirit to dwell in our hearts and teach us this attitude of letting go. Without that Spirit we could not undertake to overcome the Forsyte in us. On the one hand Jesus makes it difficult. He sets up a serious challenge to the possessiveness of mankind. His Gospel does not compromise on the spirit of poverty.* But on the other hand Jesus gives us the Holy Spirit to assist us. To meet the challenge of a hard Gospel, we have the powerful energy of God within us. We need it. Without the assistance of the Holy Spirit we would not be able to be poor. It is one of those areas in us where the wind and the fire are needed most.

Christians have to be clear where they stand with regard to property and goods. They should not condemn them, since they are good things. But they should be ruthless and radical towards the possessive instinct in themselves. There Christ asks for everything and rejects any compromise – surely because the facts of the case themselves reject compromise. If I do not act ruthlessly against my possessiveness, I will be possessed by it. It will lead me and govern me. I will be caught up in an unending spiral of desire, fulfilment and greater desire and soon both my surrender to God and my openness to my neighbour will have been thrown aside. In fact those two Gospel commands of love presuppose an attitude of poverty and detachment from self which are incompatible with the acquisitive spirit. Perhaps the reason we so often fail to love as we should is not because of a defect of loving in us, but because we are unwilling to conquer our spirit of

* Though the official Church has, frequently.

greed and so, inevitably, put ourselves before others. When it comes to a final count we cling to our own self's needs and put our neighbour second. This is true of families as well as individuals.

The surrender to God in adoration and to one's neighbour in availability imply a 'letting go' which is the opposite of the acquisitive 'hanging on'. We have to be very honest with ourselves about the possessive instinct. Unless we root it out from the depths, it will take charge and oust every fine feeling in our hearts and leave only selfish concern. Jesus really meant it when he said 'You cannot serve God and Mammon'. Surely the saddest failure of christians to follow Christ has been over this teaching on poverty. Non-christians in the Third World learn about the teaching of Christ on poverty and then experience shock over the conduct of christians who visit their country for commercial gain. Is it an accident, they ask. that in the whole world the 'Haves' who have cornered the world's resources come from the christian part of the globe, and the 'Have-nots' who are exploited live in the non-christian part? Where does Christ stand on that issue? How seriously have his followers taken the Sermon on the Mount?

I once spent two days with a family. The husband held a good academic job in a university. He had, however, just refused a much longed for promotion in his department because promotion when it came depended on a serious compromise of principle. The decision was not taken lightly. He talked it over with his wife and they prayed about it. In the end they made their choice, even though it meant his being passed over in favour of younger, less scrupulous, men, and even though it affected the education of their children. What impressed me most about the weekend was the atmosphere of peace, joy and liberation in the household. A decision for the Gospel's sake had been taken, a decision for poverty and a relative obscurity with Christ, instead of more money and departmental fame without Christ. The result was a visible liberation of the Spirit in the family, a real abandoning of ambition and possessiveness in favour of christian freedom. The Holy Spirit was tangibly present. The lad who refused the job in the firm which made immoral drugs had a responsibility only to himself aged 21. Here was a family man with ties and responsibilities who had faced the challenge of Jesus' teaching and said yes, however difficult that yes was. The result was a marvellous serenity and joy in his home.

Christ's call to us to be poor in spirit is a call to say an unconditional yes to the Father. So often we want to say 'yes-but', and in that 'but' is contained all the conditions we would like to make in our surrender to the Father. We want to please God and do his will, but – we must also have prosperity, good health, a good reputation, material security. We find it hard to let go and leave those concerns to God. We want to make demands, stake out conditions around our abandonment. The Spirit given to us then teaches us the lesson promulgated by Job that the only thing to do is to serve God without conditions, whether serving him leads to prosperity or disaster, the secure, well-heated farmhouse or the dunghill. What matters is God's service; everything else is conditional to that. Jesus summed this up in a beautiful phrase: 'Where your treasure is, there your heart will be.' In other words, for the follower of Christ it is a question of perspective. Our ultimate treasure is God. All other treasures are short term. Being poor in spirit means lengthening our perspectives so much that we keep our eye always on our ultimate treasure which is God and so can be carefree and detached (like the lilies of the field) about the short term treasures. In the long perspective they are not important. That is an easy sentiment to air. The saints appear in our midst and prove by their lives how difficult (but how liberating) it is to live it. Usually they are extraordinarily ordinary persons making no fuss as they choose God and reject Mammon. Being ordinary and extraordinary at the same time is their way of being sacraments of Christ's poverty in the world.

I confess that it is easier to promote the general principles of Jesus Christ concerning poverty of spirit than to lay down a programme of action for particular individuals. The landowner, the capitalist, the professional man, the middle-class family – they all possess property, sometimes in plenty. (They do not always think so. It is surprising how many rich people tell you they are poor.) How does Christ mean them to act about their property and money? Ultimately this is a private matter for each conscience, and there is no clear-cut path of action in each case. But there is one neglected element which I would look for in all christian property-holding. This is the element of sharing. If possessions are shared, inequality of capital and income (which it is impossible, anyway to prevent) does not matter much. Houses, possessions, motorcars, private ground, although they 'belong' in law to one person or family can be made freely available to those who cannot have them. Privacy can be abolished in favour of hospitality. Trespassers need not be prosecuted but welcomed. The truly warm mark of the christian family could become the open house, with no barriers of class, creed, colour or privilege to prevent outsiders becoming insiders. This, I suggest, is the christian way ahead in our capitalist society with its built-in divide between haves and have-nots. Legislation towards communism by itself will not usher in christian living. It has no effect on the cupidity of man. But a freely shared, practical communism could act as a beacon for the future. There are some homes which already practise this open christianity. Like the first christians the impact of Christ's teaching upon them has made them not hoard the good things of creation for themselves but share them. The more we in our families share what we have with all who come, the lighter hearted and freer we will be – like the birds of the air and the flowers of the field.

## Chapter 19

## Love and the Status Quo

In an earlier chapter I spoke of Jesus Christ's love for all men and how it led him to break through the taboo-barriers erected by the society of his day. By taking love seriously he found himself criticising, at least by his actions, the established social system of his day. Not out of youthful pride or aged malice, but because he wanted men to be free to love everyone, he came into conflict with the rulers of society. They eventually could not stand his criticism and put him to death. It was a death due to love or, as he put it, a 'love unto death'. It is rather frightening to read that he left a command for all of his followers to love each other 'as I have loved you'. Together with this demanding standard of love, however, he sent us the Spirit Counsellor to teach us and aid us in living up to that high standard. In our hearts the Holy Spirit is present to urge us to maintain that high standard and accept nothing less as christianity. Christ places sanctity as the aim before our eyes, but pours his Spirit into our hearts to help us achieve it.

All through christian history there have been compromises made both by individuals and by the Church to water down this christian standard of love. Once again the saints have been there taking Christ's command literally, so raising the standards once again to those set by Jesus. The saints have never been content with the second best and have always worked for the complete gospel. At the very beginning some of the first christian leaders wanted out of caution to impose the Jewish Law and circumcision upon the Gentile converts to the Christian Way, but St Paul was there to say that no such barriers need be erected since faith in Christ was sufficient for salvation. No security was needed other than a bold faith in Jesus Christ. In 14th century Italy most christians were ready to accept the unlovely situation of the Pope conducting business from exile in Avignon, but Catherine of Siena knew that this was a compromise and, astonishingly, succeeded in reversing the situation. In Tudor England the English bishops accepted the ecclesiastical compromise imposed on them by Henry VIII for less than christian reasons. Like many bishops since, they were great men for 'prudence'. But John Fisher, Bishop of Rochester refused to accept the compromise and so was sent to his death. In the last war most German christians compromised with the Nazi regime – 'obedience' demanded it. But brave men like Bonhoeffer did not. They could not compromise on their christian principles of love and justice. God knows what it costs holy people to take their following of Christ so literally. It is that inner abandon to the Father which prompts them to do so and accept no easy compromise.

Twenty years ago catholics were brought up on the spiritual doctrine of duties of state. The devout follower of Christ found himself in a certain state of life. Holiness for him consisted in living in that state of life and carrying out its duties with christian zeal. The priest aimed at being the perfect priest; the layman at being the perfect layman – if he was a duke, then a holy duke, if a dustman, a holy dustman. This practice received apparent impetus from the teaching of St Thérèse of Lisieux with her doctrine of the Little Way. Whatever your state in life you could be a saint and, in fact, were called to be a saint. It was not so much what you did but the love with which you did it, that pleased God. Nothing was too small to be outside God's plan. You could pick up a pin for the love of God and so contribute to the life of the Church and the salvation of the world. This doctrine of the Little Way helped enormous numbers of simple, unimportant people. It gave deep christian meaning to many drab lives. Consequently St Thérèse was instinctively canonised by the people before she was canonised by Pope Pius XI.

In one thing, however, the doctrine of duties of state is deficient. It presupposes that the 'state' people find themselves in is given, i.e. is part of God's plan. Once this is presupposed the doctrine follows logically. If God placed you in a particular state, then sanctity consists in staying there and loving God. In other words, the 'duties of state' doctrine proposes no criticism of the status quo, no attempt to christianise the society itself which establishes the various states of life. It is a spirituality for a static world with fixed positions in society and no possibility of changing them. Dukes were dukes, factory workers were factory workers; rich men lived comfortably, poor men lived uncomfortably. The duty of state was clear for each member of society: to accept his lot and be holy in that acceptance. It was the spirituality of post-tridentine Europe, of the *ancien régime* where positions in Church and State were fixed and did not change. It was a spirituality especially suitable for the recusant catholics of England debarred from positions in society and the Irish immigrant catholics exiled in an unwelcoming Britain.

Nowadays we would accept all that is good in the spirituality of duties of state, but we would add that faithfully following Christ involves also a duty to criticise society and question the status quo. Christ did this in his time and so was unpopular. We, in following him, are expected to do the same and, perhaps also be unpopular. But Christ was a 'disturber' and a revolutionary not for political ends but simply out of love for all men. We, prompted by the Holy Spirit, have to aim at the same priorities: first love God and men, then change society, when that love demands it. Holy people get this priority right. Thérèse of Lisieux is a case in point. She started off by determining to carry out her duties of state perfectly, but her burning love of God led her to see that changes in the traditional spirituality were needed and as novice mistress she inaugurated a new, more merciful, teaching under the very nose of her prioress. In the small world of her Carmel it was revolutionary, and since her death has transformed catholic spirituality. Thérèse was, in fact, no accepter of the status quo. Her abandonment to the Father urged her to take new and not always popular initiatives. The revolutionising pattern of sanctity worked itself out in her too.

The instinct to criticise the role imposed on us by society, in other words the refusal merely to accept a given status quo, is called 'ecstasy' by sociologists. They call it that because it involves a 'standing outside' the given pattern of society. In order to look upon your role in a community objectively you have mentally to stand outside it, taking up a position of 'ec-stasis'. The use of this word is significant for a believer in God, for it is the word he uses for one who is drawn out of himself towards God by an overpowering force. To fall into an ecstasy is to be caught up beyond yourself in God. This makes the point of this chapter. Impelled by the force of the Holy Spirit within him, the saint is caught up into a state of ecstasy before God. From this special position he can look at the world he belongs to and make a unique criticism concerning it. Time and again in history the saints have done that. In this they have imitated their master who after his baptism by John went to the desert to pray. In the course of his forty days of fasting and prayer before God he sorted out what his mission was to be. After resisting the three fake notions of it, proposed to him by the Devil, he came back into society and proclaimed the Kingdom of God. His vision of the Kingdom stemmed from his 'ec-stasis' before the Father. There was no political opportunism in it or personal ambition. He had seen what the will of the Father was, and now set himself to obey it, regardless of the personal dangers which culminated in his death, and regardless of the social misunderstanding which constituted him a 'failure'. It was for all ages a lesson about how the love of God taken seriously affects not only the personal life of the individual, but also the status quo of society.

## Chapter 20

## Fall, Gall Themselves

The old lives of the saints made much of suffering. They dwelt especially on the physical sufferings which the holy men and women imposed on themselves. We read of monks who stood up to their neck in freezing water all night, of nuns who wore sharp chains next to their skin all day. As we go further back in time to the monks of the Egyptian desert there is a flavour of the *Guinness Book of Records* about the penitential feats of the holy men and women of the Early Church. (Though there is none of that spirit in the New Testament.) What are we to make of it all today?

The lesson being promulgated by the old hagiographers, in their sometimes crude way, is the lesson of suffering: it is, first of all, inescapable in this life, but, secondly, it is valuable and does us good, if we take it in the right way. What the saints realised was that to take the following of Christ seriously in this world lands those who do it in suffering. Christian discipleship leads us into conflict with the world. This inevitably entails suffering. The saints welcomed this, not because they wanted to suffer or thought suffering was a good in itself, but because it was a badge, a sign that they were taking Christ seriously or better still, that Christ was taking them seriously and allowing them to suffer in his cause. St Ignatius of Antioch in the first century writes of looking forward to being the Lord's wheat ground into flour by the teeth of the wild beasts in the arena, and lyrically welcomes this suffering and death. He turns martyrdom into a kind of mysticism. It makes us a bit uncomfortable today. It sounds too physical. But people like St Ignatius were not being masochistic. They were overcome with love of Jesus Christ to whom they were witnessing; they dwelt on the sufferings which their witness involved only because of their love for him. Their eyes were fixed on the meeting with Christ in heaven which they longed for. The intermediate pain involved in getting there was secondary but in their view important.

We do well to remember that christianity did not invent suffering. Suffering was already in the world since time began. Christianity worked out a creative way of handling it: to fight against it when it is unnecessary, but to accept it lovingly when it is the way to do Christ's will. Christianity thus gave a meaning to suffering. The meaning is not that suffering is good in itself but that, in God's providence, it is an opportunity to love – the supreme test in many instances. (Our love can often be only a matter of words until it is tested by suffering.) This is how Jesus accepted suffering. On the one hand he did his best to alleviate it when he could: he healed the sick and brought comfort to the distressed. But on the other hand he warned his disciples of the inevitability of suffering for themselves if they were to embrace his gospel. And so he said that disciples wishing to follow him would have to take up the cross daily as part of their discipleship. In Gethsemane he showed them how to take up the cross creatively. He at first sought to avoid it, but then accepted it when he knew it was his Father's will. He thus gave a meaning to suffering by concentrating on the love behind it. The

117

abandonment of the Son to the Father, not the whips, the nails or the soldier's spear, is the real instrument of our Redemption. The Father responded to this dedication by raising Jesus from the dead. What is new in the New Testament is not, therefore, the Cross, which is as old as time, but the loving acceptance of it, which led to the Resurrection. The Resurrection is the sign that God accepts suffering performed in love, and crowns such a death with life.

The significant sufferings in the life of a christian are not those which he manufactures for himself (mortifications) but those which life sends him. There is profound truth in Jesus' words to Peter after the Resurrection:

'I tell you most solemnly,
when you were young
you put on your own belt
and walked where you liked;
but when you grow old
you will stretch out your hands
and somebody else will put a belt round you
and take you where you would rather not go.'

(Jn 21:18)

Girding ourselves with our own belt is how we all begin, and even when we meet suffering in doing so, there remains a certain thrill in being in charge of our destiny. In a subtle way it builds up our ego. Maturity comes when someone else girds us and takes us off in a direction of his choice, and all we are asked to do is to show ourselves ready to follow by 'stretching out our hands'. There is more suffering involved in this because it is less dramatic and does nothing to build up our pride. It is the

118

sort of Cross which Jesus embraced. Placed there by somebody else (but 'meant' by the Father) and accepted creatively for the sake of the Kingdom. There is nothing for the book of records in this. But for God there is the growth of a loving heart in the disciple. When such a death is accepted in a spirit of abandonment to the Father there is a point to it, and resurrection follows.

Holy people show us how to live through these deaths and so attain resurrection of the spirit. It is their special contribution to mankind. We imperfect followers can learn from them – not by taking sufferings upon ourselves unnecessarily but by seeing the hand of God behind our necessary sufferings and resolving to meet each 'death' with love. That way lies resurrection because we commune with the Father in each acceptance.

One kind of death which people in the 20th century face with frequency is the death involved in change. In many areas of life today rapid change is taking place. Socially, culturally, religiously, old established and loved ways are dying before our eyes. They are frequently replaced by new, brash, unlovely substitutes. Worse still, they are sometimes replaced by nothing settled; things are left 'open-ended' and for ever temporary. This can be death to someone who loved the old ways and depended for security upon them. It would be possible to take examples from any segment of life: the death of the English village, the death of the family firm, the death of the tenement communities in our cities, the death of the family doctor. All these involve suffering for the tra- ditional minded. For the purpose of this book, the death of the pre-Vatican II Catholic Church is a significant example.

Pre-Vatican catholic culture with its certainties and

securities, its ordered religious relations, confident literature, beautiful latin liturgy, has died. This has brought
genuine hurt, the Cross, to many catholics. It is not,
however, an accidental death. Quite clearly, it is 'meant' by
the Father. The way to holiness for us is therefore through
(not round) the ruins of the old culture. It lies through
accepting the hurt involved, not in escaping from it. In
our generation God has administered a holy jolt to us all
and asked us to participate in an exodus away from the
perhaps over-complacent security of the old ways of being
a catholic out in the desert of the uncertain new ways. It
is, of course, possible to argue for or against many of the
particular changes which are being made. In fact we
ought to exercise our discernment in every situation and
never accept change for the sake of change. The point,
however, is that we are being asked to change, and to
accept the mental pain involved. As always in following
Christ, we have to undergo a kind of death in order to
live more fully in him. Or, to put it the other way round,
the price of new catholic vigour is the death of old
catholic strength. Many priests have found, for instance,
that they only made the new liturgy work vigorously in
their parishes when they and their people had once and
for all given up hankering after the strengths involved in
the old liturgy.

Far more potent and painful than the deaths found in
ecclesial life are the inner deaths of the spiritual life. Here
again one could pick out a number of areas of the inner
life where painful suffering happens. In the end, I think,
they all would come under that heading 'death of self'
coined by the spiritual masters to explain this happening.

The collapse of self-confidence is a painful death. We
go along at our job, in our life, in our christianity, and we

have confidence in God and ourselves. We live with the unexamined expectation that we will mostly succeed at what we try and that our relationships will go well. There will be inevitable ups and downs, but on the whole we will be accepted by those we meet. Consequently we accept ourselves deep down as worthwhile even when we do not think about it much. Then one day this comes to an end. We find that we do not accept ourselves as worthwhile. Our self-confidence evaporates like the mist and we are suffused with the feelings of being worthless. We feel no good, hollow, a sham, harmful to those we have dealings with. It is not really possible to put this nameless mood of despair and self-hate into words. Once on paper the mood looks tame. It is not in reality. It is desperately lonely and frightening to feel worthless and unaccepted by anyone. It is to live in a sort of fog which cuts us off from other men and women. (They seem so confident and happy in their lives.) This fog permeates every corner of the mind. It tends to smother every creative thought and extinguish the spontaneous sparks of hope which life provides. When it is there we can look on nothing with pleasure. The best we can do is drag ourselves round our duties empty of pleasure in them. We fly blind and full of fears. There is no experienced point in what we do. Relationships only provide fear in the stomach and disgust with self. We experience the collapse of hope and are beset with fears we have never felt before.

The mood has no time limit. It can last a day, but, most terribly, it can last years. This is because it is not susceptible to being changed from the outside. Evidence of success will, apparently, not alter the feeling of failure, because the mind has an answer for every scrap of evidence: the success is sham, or, I played no part in it –

it was luck. The despairing thing is the inability to think our way out of this state. The mind, suffused with self-depreciation, does not accept evidence which goes against the mood. Next year the same set of facts may well produce euphoria and brimming confidence. This year we are drained dry of hope. Even the facts of success only cause humiliation; we have played no part in it except to cause hindrance. What others say in order to help also has no effect. We recognise the sympathy but what is said to assist or clarify does not do so. Internally there is just a great emptiness. On all four sides of the emptiness are the 'mountains, cliffs of fall', spoken of by the poet. It is not pleasant to hang there. Hanging there we know that the abyss below is not really empty, but we still hang there, numb.

There are, of course, psychological explanations for these moods when they happen – self-hate, repressed anger, perhaps. But there is also the spiritual explanation: it is part of the purpose of God. It is the death of self-confidence in order to bring to birth an ever deeper, genuine lasting confidence in God. It is the lesson of the exodus again – this time in terms of leaving behind our purely natural self-confidence in favour of a new spiritual trust in God, forged in the desert. God is leading us in the desert with a purpose – the purpose of weaning us from dependence on ourselves or any human authority. He wants us to depend on a deeper source than our own strength, namely himself. The weaning process is painful because it attacks the roots of our self-confidence. We do not easily admit failure at that level. We have to be overcome by immense feelings of despair before we ask for help, let alone give in to God. We are brought to doubt our whole possession of self. In this way God teaches us to depend on him only. We have to fly blind. relying on God. It is not easy. It brings no pleasure or felt certitude, but it is the way to resurrection. It teaches us to ask about the right questions: not about personal effort, success or failure, but about the will of God. When resurrection takes place, death is seen to have a point. But the next time it happens it is no less frightening. By these rehearsals of death and resurrection the Father draws us forward to the crisis of our final death, when the only question that matters will be concerning the will of God. If we learn to respond generously at these moments, our faith tells us we will be led through to resurrection and joy.

## Chapter 21

# And Gash Gold-Vermilion

Holiness comes when we can be *immediate*. This can only happen when the 'death of self' has begun to take place. Until that is under way, we still have the tendency to focus attention on our reactions to life instead of life itself. While we are still focussing on our reactions to life, we are not simple. We are varied, because anxious about ourselves. We find ourselves caught up in a circle of anxiety, which is difficult to break out of, and which leads us round and round into further complications. When we meet people we are preoccupied with ourselves, how we are 'going over', what image we are projecting, whether we are being accepted, whether we are helping them or not. When we pray we are preoccupied with our prayer, how it is going, what sort it is, whether it is genuine or not.

Holiness comes when we have achieved immediacy and in our encounters bump up against the Other. Meeting people we become quickly sensitive to them, preoccupied with their needs, anxious about them. We experience a liberation from pre-occupations with self and wake to the marvellous rich variety in other people. Their sorrows and anxieties distress us much and we weep with them when they weep. But we also rejoice with them in their joys and thrill with them in their ambitions. There is no limit to the rich experience of meeting other people when no personal worries get in the way. There is enormous variety in the lives of other people. Being sensitive to them introduces us to new worlds of interest and love and laughter.

In all this we have reached a level which can be called 'simple' because there are few inhibitions between us and the rest of the world. In fact the rich variety we experience in other people is made possible by the simplicity in us. People who are anxious about their relationships do not make many new ones. They cannot afford to take on new anxieties, so they limit their meetings with other people in complex ways. People who are simple with God are not preoccupied or anxious about their success or failure with people, so they tend to make new friends all the time. It is not that they succeed all the time and never fail. It is that they do not think in those categories. In their relationships they are concerned with others, not with their own record, so they carry on, happy in their immediacy. This usually guarantees them success with people, but they accept both success and failure with serenity.

The source of their serenity is another, deeper immediacy: their immediacy with God. In the heart of their being they face God and abandon themselves to him. They are not preoccupied with 'prayer', only with God. He occupies them fully, because he now appears as the Reality of all realities. They recognise that the initiative is no longer with them, but with God. They no longer seek him out, because they have found him. He will never leave them, and they know they will never leave him. In the ground of their being they sink and merge with God. There are no longer two presences: God to them, they to God: but one presence only, a mutual immediacy.

This immediacy is felt in terms of place and time. God is felt to be 'here'. He is present, a spiritual existence, in this place. God is also felt to be 'now'. He is present, at this time. No laborious process is needed to find God or make him relevant. He is known to be present, here and now. In de Caussade's phrase he is the 'sacrament of the present moment'. Every created being is then seen to receive its relevance from God, not vice versa. A Copernican revolution thus takes place. When we set out to serve God we begin by placing him on the boundary of our consciousness. We ascertain that he exists, then admit him to our world, then adore him. But it is not really like that. God is not in our world. We are in his. He is at the centre, we are on the circumference. He admits us into his world. He is supremely relevant. The proper question is: are *we*? If we are, it is because God creates us and places us in the world. We get our relevance from him. He places us. We are not the centre. He is. Realising this involves a spiritual revolution. When the realisation dawns in prayer, everything falls into place, and is seen to be very simple. We have arrived at a condition of simplicity.

The soul brims over with the presence of God, and this brings joy. There is joy in being alive, joy in being created and loved by God, joy in God being God! There is even joy in suffering, and in the deaths which God sends us before each resurrection. Perhaps the most particular form the joy takes is thanks. Giving thanks is a happy task. There is always much joy in saying thank you to people who have helped us. How much more is there joy when it is God whom we are thanking! Saying thanks to human beings is never more than intermittent, because the services they perform for us are intermittent. With

God it is gloriously different, because we have something to thank him for all the time: our existence, our christian discipleship, our friends and families, the episodes of our life, creation itself. Above all we have to thank God for himself for being God! Thanking God, therefore, need never cease. It is, in fact, a lifetime's task, which is why christian discipleship at its most profound level develops into this mixture of joy and thanks which never comes to an end.

Being sad contracts our hearts, but when we are thankful they expand with joy. Thanks and praise go together – they are expansive movements. So the condition of simplicity, when we know God to be here and now, and rest in gratitude, is a joyful and expansive condition. God's presence, and our being accepted by him, and the world's existence, including especially other people's – these are why we praise God and are joyful. Suffering is in our life; it is interwoven in all we do. But suffering does not impede the joy and thanks, because we know that it is part of a plan which brings redemption out of pain, resurrection out of death. This mysterious plan, or 'passover mystery', is akin to the cycle of sowing and reaping in the fields. It is the pattern of the grain of wheat which has to go through its period of dying as a necessary preliminary to its growth as corn in the spring. This cycle of death and life in the fields is full of joy, as Psalm 126 sings:

> Those who are sowing in tears
> will sing when they reap.
> They go out, they go out, full of tears,
> carrying seed for the sowing:
> they come back, they come back, full of song,
> carrying their sheaves.

Saints are people who recognise this cycle of death and resurrection not merely as a theoretical truth, but actually, by living it. For them the passover mystery is a reality which they live, and so the joy and thanks bound up in it are actualities you see in their faces and experience in meeting them. Saints are happy persons who have suffered on their way to that fulfilment of joy. As they carry home their sheaves they are full of song. With Mother Julian of Norwich in the midst of this world of pain they are rejoicing because All shall be well, and all manner of thing shall be well. They have seen the point and found the meaning of existence. So they praise God all the time. The coming together in their experience of the fire of suffering and the rose of love in a condition of complete simplicity makes them sing for joy.